Nouns & Verbs

ALSO BY

CAMPBELL McGRATH

XX: Poems for the Twentieth Century

In the Kingdom of the Sea Monkeys

Shannon: A Poem of the Lewis and Clark Expedition

Seven Notebooks

Pax Atomica

Florida Poems

Road Atlas

Spring Comes to Chicago

American Noise

Capitalism

Nouns & Verbs

New and Selected Poems

CAMPBELL McGRATH

An Imprint of HarperCollins*Publishers*

HarperCollins books may be purchased for educational, business, or sales promotional use. For information, please email the Special Markets Department at SPsales@harpercollins.com.

FIRST EDITION

Designed by Suet Yee Chong

Library of Congress Cataloging-in-Publication Data has been applied for.

ISBN 978-0-06-285414-8

19 20 21 22 23   LSC   10 9 8 7 6 5 4 3 2 1

To Daniel Halpern

CONTENTS

2. Poems

3. Prose Poems

4. An Odyssey of Appetite

5. Poems

Preface

Poets may inhabit a realm of words, but they remain closet numerologists. Perhaps it's a vestigial memory of counting syllables in all those lines of iambic pentameter, but ten seems like a significant number, and so ten books feels like a milepost worth pausing beside, a place to assess, examine, parse, and reassemble. Thus this book, which surveys thirty-five years of writing (the most recent poems were written in 2016, the oldest in 1981), though only eight of my ten previous collections are actually represented here. *Shannon: A Poem of the Lewis and Clark Expedition* is a book-length poem that feels complete unto itself, while *XX: Poems for the Twentieth Century* is too recently published to need revisiting. Longer poems are simply harder to accommodate, and so "The Bob Hope Poem" is represented by only a single section, while works such as "The Florida Poem" and "Dawn Notebook" are absent altogether.

The mandate of such a collection, as I see it, is to offer a hint of where you are going while charting the territory already explored. Accordingly, the first of this book's five sections is composed of new poems, written over the past six or seven years, in a variety of shapes and sizes. In the hopes of creating a book that harmonizes with, but does not echo, the originals, I have organized older poems by form rather than chronology: there are two sections of lyric poems, a lengthy set of prose poems, and a sequence of longer poems reconstituted as an episodic personal epic, "An Odyssey of Appetite," which explores America's limitless material and spiritual hungers. If anything has obsessed my creative impulse to date, surely it is this. There is also a scattering of uncollected poems, happy to have found a home at last. *Nouns & Verbs* is just that, I hope—not a greatest-hits collection but a new house sheltering some familiar residents, a book that stands on its own solid foundation, unbothered by a few termites in its beams or a little rain seeping in around the windows.

Acknowledgments

Poems from *American Noise, Spring Comes to Chicago, Road Atlas, Florida Poems, Pax Atomica, Seven Notebooks,* and *In the Kingdom of the Sea Monkeys* reprinted by permission of the author and Ecco.

Poems from *Capitalism* reprinted by permission of the author.

The new poems in this volume have previously appeared in the following publications, whose editors I thank:

5 a.m., Arts & Letters, The Atlantic, Colorado Review, Cortland Review, Floating Wolf Quarterly, Jai-Alai Magazine, Kenyon Review, La Presa, Miami Rail, Michigan Quarterly Review, Margie, New England Review, The New Yorker, Pivot, Ploughshares, Plume, Poem-a-Day, Poetry, Salmagundi, South Florida Poetry Journal, Utsanga, and *Witness.*

"Saying No" was produced as a limited-edition broadside by Tom Virgin, and "Cryptozoology" was produced as a limited-edition broadside by Andrew Reid, both as part of the Sweat Broadside Collaboration in Miami.

A musical version of "Pentatina for Five Vowels," by jazz composer Dan Peter Sundland, can be found on his 2013 album, *Elevenette,* while recorded versions of several of these poems can be found online, at the Poetry Foundation website, among others.

The inscription for Part Four, on page 163, is from "Infinite Needs," the rest of which can be found in *Pax Atomica.*

Among many such obligations, "Birds and Trees" is indebted to Pablo Neruda's rhetorical verve, "Sleepwork" owes its form to Terrance Hayes's dexterous imagination, and "Reading Emily Dickinson at Jiffy Lube" tips its cap to the titling strategy of Ariel Francisco.

Part One

New Poems

SAYING NO

No sir, absolutely not, sorry, but no.
Not sorry, actually—just no.
Keep it simple, plain vanilla: nope.
Not happening. Big en, big oh.

No way, no how.
Negative, nuh-uh, ixnay, *nyet*.
No no, no no.
No-no-no-no-no-no-no.

Not likely, not likely. Maybe,
but I doubt it.
Possibly, conceivably, in theory.
Un-huh, mm-hmm. . . .

Well yeah, sure, okay, why not,
oh definitely, yes,
wow, I mean anything,
anything at all, when can we begin?

PENTATINA FOR FIVE VOWELS

Today is a trumpet to set the hounds baying.
The past is a fox the hunters are flaying.
Nothing unspoken goes without saying.
Love's a casino where lovers risk playing.
The future's a marker our hearts are prepaying.

The future's a promise there's no guaranteeing.
Today is a fire the field mice are fleeing.
Love is a marriage of feeling and being.
The past is a mirror for wishful sightseeing.
Nothing goes missing without absenteeing.

Nothing gets cloven except by dividing.
The future is chosen by atoms colliding.
The past's an elision forever eliding.
Today is a fog bank in which I am hiding.
Love is a burn forever debriding.

Love's an ascent forever plateauing.
Nothing is granted except by bestowing.
Today is an anthem the cuckoos are crowing.
The future's a convolute river onflowing.
The past is a lawn the neighbor is mowing.

The past is an answer not worth pursuing.
Love is only won by wooing.
The future's a climax forever ensuing.
Nothing gets done except by the doing.
Today is a truce between reaping and ruing.

A GREETING ON THE TRAIL

Turning fifty, at last I come to understand,
belatedly, unexpectedly, and quite suddenly,
that poetry is not going to save anybody's life,
least of all my own. Nonetheless I choose to believe
the journey is not a descent but a climb,
as when, in a forest of golden-green morning sunlight,
one sees another hiker on the trail, who calls out,
Where are you bound, friend, to the valley or the mountaintop?
Many things—seaweed, pollen, attention—drift.
News of the universe's origin infiltrates atom by atom
the oxygenated envelope of the atmosphere.
My sense of purpose vectors away on rash currents
like the buoys I find tossed on the beach after a storm,
cork bobbers torn from old crab traps.
And what befalls the woebegotten crabs,
caged and forgotten at the bottom of the sea?
Are the labors to which we are summoned by dreams
so different from the tasks to which sunlight
enslaves us? One tires of niceties. We sleep now
surrounded by books, books piled in heaps
by the bedside, stacked along the walls of the room.
Let dust accrue on their spines and colophons.
Let their ragged towers rise and wobble.
Of course the Chinese poets were familiar with all this,
T'ao Ch'ien, Hsieh Ling-yün, Po Chü-i,
masterful sophisticates adopting common accents
for their nostalgic drinking songs, their laments
to age and temple ruins and imperial avarice,
autumn leaves caught in a tumbling stream.
As the river flows at the urging of gravity, as a flower
blooms after April rain, we are implements
of the unseen, always working for someone else.
The boss is a tall woman in a sky-blue shirt

or a man with one thumb lost to a crosscut saw
or science or art or the Emperor, what matter?
We scrabble within the skin of time
like mice in the belly of a boa constrictor,
Jonah within Leviathan, pacing the keel, rib to rib,
surrounded by the pulse of that enormous, compassionate heart.
Later we dance in orchards of guava and lychee nuts
to the shifting registers of distant music,
a clattering of plates as great fish are lifted from the grill,
seared black with bitter orange and lemongrass.
Orchid trees bloom here, Tulip trees and Flame trees,
but no Idea trees, no trees of Mercy,
for these are human capacities, human occasions.
Because it has about it something of the old village magic,
the crop made to rise by seed of words,
by spell or incantation—
because it frightens and humbles us to recall
our submission to such protocols—
for this do we fear poetry, for the unresolved darkness
of the past. *Where are you bound, friend,*
on this bright and fruitful morning—to the valley
or the mountaintop? To the mountaintop.

MY MUSIC

My music belongs to me and it is awesome.

My music is way better than your music,
your music is trash, garbage stench
of a hot summer night behind the dumpsters at Taco Bell,
rancid, but I'm there, too, drinking beers
in the parking lot with the windows down
and the radio tuned to a baseball game
we are following as casually
as the stars' erratic flight plan—that music
is my music, all of it, ball game, laughter of friends
and the crack of frosty six-packs,
asphalt returning the day's heat to the sky.

My music is so much better than your music
I pity you—almost I would pity you
if I were not disgusted by your chump-change music.
My music will beat your music to a pulp.
My music will turn your music into a car wash
run by infants—their tiny hands
can't even hold the sponges!
They will never, ever degrease those tire rims!

Get out of my business with that nightmare
you call music, with your tears
and pleading, the whining of excuses—oh, sorry,
that is your music,
that crybaby boohoo-ery,
that blurt, that diminuendo, that waaah,
that large-ass mess,
that chicken potpie all pocked with freezer burn,
that coyote hung from a fence post as a trophy and a caution.

My music cannot be muted or dimmed,
it cannot be labeled, disciplined, contained
by manicured hedges, my music
is the untamed wilderness of the soul,
the rebar that holds up the skyscrapers of your city is my music,
watch out, your city will crumble to rubble without it,
but don't worry, it wasn't much to begin with,
that place you called home
with its measling river, its rusty bridges,
there's a carnival in the meadow of the old floodplain,
cotton candy and whirligig lights and the racket
rising up from the carousel
is my music,

old guys fishing along the breakwater,
coffee can half-full of fat, wriggling night crawlers—
that worm-thrum,
that earth-mouth-echo is my music.

The trinket in the bottom of the Cracker Jack box is mine,
the Employee of the Month parking space is mine,

I am the little golden man on your bowling trophy,
I am the nickels collected in your old pickle jars,
I am the U-Haul pulling out of the driveway, leaving
your town forever—goodbye, Loserville,

hello, New Hampshire, Alabama, Montana, Texas,

I am all those places, everywhere
you ever dreamed of going
I have been there and pissed on the phone poles already,
I am the names of all fifty states on your tongue,

their Olde English nostalgia and Amerindian prolixity
and majuscule Latinate transliterations rolled together,

I own the alphabet and the stars in the sky,

I own the pigeons sleeping beneath the overpasses
and the shadows of pine trees
and the corn husks in a paper bag on the porch
and the ants on the bottle of barbecue sauce,
ants all over the cupcakes and watermelon wedges,
huge black carpenter ants and raspberry crazy ants
and the almost invisible warp-speed ants
like cartoon swashbucklers of the microsphere,

the footfall of the ants is my music, oh yes,
cacophonous, euphonious, that tumult, that mad march,
louder than circus elephants
and softer than flowers opening, gentler
than apple blossoms descending into creek water,

petals falling—one,
two,
three, four.

BIRDS AND TREES

I'm tired of not being a great blue whale.
I'm sick of frills and gossamer ostinatos.
I want to feed a Happy Meal to a cheetah.
I'm tired of not being Nicanor Parra.
I want to say, basically, fuck you to poetry
with all its outlandish maunderings.

Magic numbers piss me off,
I'm bored by rubrics and party lines,
the bloody giblets of nostalgia disgust me.
The *past* is a sadly inadequate word
for what we've been through,
earthly existence, this life, right here.

Nature ruled the planet long before our entrance
yet surely its reign was nothing more
than a pulsating machine-works of appetite,
ultra-vivid but purely mechanical,
a rococo cuckoo clock
trivialized by its own clownish reality,
its too literal presence in the moment.

Is the air in which they disport
truly so wonderful, vainglorious swallows
making a spectacle of themselves
as if to prove their familiarity with a drama
in which we resemble minor characters
bumbling onstage in the final act?

Of course we admire the birds and trees
but their diffidence insults our dignity
and when, inevitably, we lash out in anger,
nature has none but herself to blame,

for we, too, bear the mark of her flawed manufacture
from our first, gasping, egg-damp cries.

To be human is to be scissor-cut
in bold strokes from imperfectly pressed paper,
our brains, like huge unblooming peonies,
tug our bodies inexorably earthward,
while language resembles a clutch of party balloons
intended to lift us to salvation
but there is so much that cannot be captured
in pink latex and self-reflective Mylar—

snow falling on the temple gardens of Kyoto,
the heroic loneliness of cemetery flags,
even our drive along the Palisades Parkway
on a summer day so long ago.

The *past*—what an awful word
for something we can never get beyond,
no matter how restlessly we travel.

The Palisades Parkway comes to an end
in Rockland County, New York,
just beyond the abandoned hamlet of Doodletown.
All good things must come to an end.
But not all good things end in Doodletown, New York.

FOUR LOVE POEMS

1. NOX BOREALIS

If Socrates drank his portion of hemlock willingly,
if the Appalachians have endured unending ages of erosion,
if the wind can learn to read our minds
and moonlight moonlight as a master pickpocket,
surely we can contend with contentment as our commission.

Deer in a stubble field, small birds dreaming
unimaginable dreams in hollow trees,
even the icicles, darling, even the icicles shame us
with their stoicism, their radiant resolve.

Listen to me now: think of something you love
but not too dearly, so the night will steal from us
only what we can afford to lose.

2. AURORA PERPETUA

O tulip, tulip, you bloom all day and later sway
a deep-waisted limbo above the dinner table,
waiting for a coin to drop into your well,
for the stars to pin your stem to their lapel.

Soon, on ocean winds, dawn cries its devotion,
our world entranced once more into being.
Let go your sumptuous rage, darling.
All this awed awakening is a form of adoration.

What's born in that fountain of salt and spume,
of spackled sea monsters and gardenia perfume,
is everything blossoming ever amounts to:
an hour of earthly nectar, a single drop of dew.

3. IMPERIUM FORTUNATUS

We were born to rule an empire together, but which one?
Empire of antique tinsel and gingerbread mansions,
of sentimental melodies on black scratchy gramophones?

Stars are piping their bossa nova rhythms
through the wires again tonight, shuffle left, shuffle right.
Even now I'm startled from a familiar dream
to chart the chords, to note the steps of passing satellites.

And then back to what was, in its way, a more perfect union.

So you see I've lost the essential distinction—
which is our dominion, darling, which the barbarian realm?
Come, I'll shed this common cloth, you slip your silken gown.
Let moonlight be our mantle, and ecstasy our crown.

4. LUX AUSTRALIS

Early evening honey and whiskey, that sweetness,
bees in the ever-blossoming tresses
of your hair, darling, the touch of a hand
like water in a parched man's cup,

the way memory chimes its silver-stringed guitar
like moonlight on a spiderweb,
milkweed stalks against rusted-out pickup trucks,
their wandering seed our only constellations,

bells in the velvet darkness before dawn,
that mystery, that consolation,
worn-down paths we walk fortified by trust in simplicity
and cans of beer in wind off the soon-to-be-planted fields.

O let us reseed the garden and eat vegetable soup
and never go to town, not even for bread.
Let us inhabit this moment forever and ever.
Live with me always in the scrap heap of my heart.

ANDROMEDA

Already the countdown has begun:
four billion years until Andromeda
collides with the Milky Way, rupturing
forever that footpath through the forest

of dreamers' jewels. I would scoff,
if I did not recall the tracery of fine hairs
swirled across an infant's skull
like the softest of inbound galaxies.

Andromeda, all your starry wonders
cannot salve the ache of baby teeth
chanced upon, this 2 A.M.,
at the bottom of a bedside drawer.

MY SADNESS

Another year is coming to an end
but my old t-shirts will not be back—

the pea-green one from Trinity College,
gunked with streaks of lawn-mower grease,

the one with orange bat wings
from Diamond Cavern, Kentucky,

vanished
without a trace.

After a two-day storm I wander the beach
admiring the ocean's lack of attachment.

I huddle beneath a seashell,
lonely as an exile.

My sadness is the sadness of water fountains.
My sadness is as ordinary as these gulls

importuning for Cheetos or scraps
of peanut butter sandwiches.

Feed them a single crust
and they will never leave you alone.

PATRIMONY

In Europe, someone is always stealing famous paintings,
as if it were so easy to dehistoricize the academy,
to sever a father's tongue and replace the past
with mute quadrilaterals of dust. Out the window

of the overnight bus maple leaves are dying in style
while the great country and western songs I love
remain baroque, sentimental and full of life.
Same tangle of grief and salvation, same wife,
same kids, same house, same city—
what changes is the book you are writing
and the faces around the table discussing the grass
Walt Whitman becomes on the earth within us.

Imagine that gallery full of stolen masterworks
and then imagine the museum of the never-created,
Schubert's slide guitar, the graphic novels of El Greco.
Imagine the movies Sappho would have made!

READING EMILY DICKINSON
AT JIFFY LUBE

Sitting in the waiting room at Jiffy Lube, reading Emily Dickinson and watching a rerun of *Matlock,* I realize that my life is exactly like this moment, when Andy Griffith turns to the jury, beaming his most grandfatherly, country-wise smile, ready to unmask the killer, and says—and says—well, they've cut to a commercial, I don't know what he says.

But then it wouldn't be much of a mystery if I did.

Anyway, I am old enough to know that guilt and innocence are relative virtues on daytime TV, and that even the present instant, with its brash odors of coffee and newspaper ink, its flocculent light, even this empire of the senses is an abiding enigma.

If I should live to be one hundred, in the year A.D. 2062, I will have seen the 200th anniversary of the *annus mirabilis* in which Emily Dickinson wrote three hundred poems while the Civil War raged at its most horrifying intensity,

and my own birth, half a century ago, will mark a fulcrum between those time-vaulting poles—

between the bloodletting at Shiloh and Antietam,

while Emily, in her solitude, penciled stanzas on scraps of wrapping paper and torn envelopes, cuttings from a landscape of fertile ingenuity, a marvelous mental garden, the undiscovered continent of the self—

and the imponderable far-off future,

when new technologies will empower us and new populations seethe with needs and the oceans shall have risen to consume this fragile sandbar on which I have injudiciously staked my claim,

and if so, this moment, right now, would mark a similar midpoint in my own life, though five more decades seems unlikely,

and I am old enough to know that I will never be Emily Dickinson.

I am old enough to recognize that justice is a prime-time fable, that the moon smiles down upon the savage and the merciful alike, old enough to understand that I will never live in the desert, which makes me sad, though I fear the desert instinctively and would never want to live there.

Still one takes comfort in imagining the contours of a life in Arizona, a life of Franciscan austerity in Bend, Oregon.

One imagines all the barrier islands and beach towns up and down the East Coast swallowed by the tantalizing waters of the Atlantic Ocean, all the taffy shops and nail salons of the Jersey Shore, the skate punks in the parking lot of the convenience store and the headbanger at the register of the convenience store and the buying of condoms and six-packs of Smirnoff Ice, a place so inimitable and ass-kicking I can already hear the pulsating guitar-and-glockenspiel intro of "Born to Run" unrolling its red carpet to my heart, a song that remains a primary text of American male identity, like *The Autobiography of Benjamin Franklin,* and being hokum, being a confection of swagger and tattered glory, subtracts nothing from its legend, and when I think of Bruce Springsteen's improbable rise to eloquence, his silent and bitter father, his bantam insecurities, his boardwalk voice and secondhand guitar, I am reminded that no act of self-expression is unrealizable here, and when I think of him now, defanged but uncorrupted, chugging through soggy Dust Bowl ballads—

as if New Jersey were not the mythic equal of Oklahoma, as if "Atlantic City" were not a folk song as potent as any of Woody Guthrie's—

well, I guess we all lose our way, sooner or later, in America,

even Bruce Springsteen.

Oh, but there was a song sung, wasn't there, eight maids a-milking and a bobtail nag, the morning after Thanksgiving and all the middle-aged stoners calling in to Z104 requesting REO Speedwagon?

There was a mystery solved, a day lived through, all sugar and oil, all lips and wind, a hat, a rabbit, a magic word.

Praise the sun's masons assembling the sensorium from photons and scraps of subatomic shadow!

Praise images that leap from the mind like ninjas!

Praise Emily Dickinson's folk-strumming daughters and Walt Whitman's fuel-injected sons—*forth-steppers from the latent unrealized baby-days!*

SAYING GOODBYE TO PAUL WALKER

My family is away for the weekend and I am home alone, cleaning out the garage, a troll-den of dust and termite wings and rusting paint cans. At five o'clock I bolt a new handle on the garage door, pop a beer, and declare victory; at seven I order in the delicious *vaca frita* from Latin Café and at ten I am drinking a bottle of Spanish wine watching *Furious 7*, the latest installment of the witless car-chase movie franchise, starring Vin Diesel, the Rock, Paul Walker, et alia, as an improbable band of maverick, shoot-'em-up, thrill-seeking auto jockeys. This episode is notable for its particularly cockamamie action sequences, general high spirits, and of course the death—in real life, just as the film had finished shooting—of Paul Walker. Watching now, it seems almost cruel to notice how earnestly and unironically square-jawed he is, which in no way distinguishes him from his current cast mates, a menagerie of hambones, blockheads, and sneering no-goodniks. Saying goodbye to Paul Walker should not be hard, and yet there was something different about him, wasn't there, a special light in his cool blue eyes, as if he were sharing a secret with us, as if he were twinkling and smirking not merely at the terrible dialogue he is compelled to utter, but at the ridiculous good fortune of his life. Saying goodbye to Paul Walker should be a piece of cake but it isn't, and though it makes no sense I've got tears in my eyes as they run a montage of farewell shots at the end of the movie—"You will always be my brother," Vin Diesel intones, v.o.—and we know that he is truly dead, that Paul Walker IV, born in Glendale in 1973, son of Cheryl and Paul III, has passed on to another plane—and yet within the movie's master narrative Paul Walker is not dead at all, he has merely "retired" and so will live forever in that phantom, cloud-lit, celluloid eternity, which is a preposterous but oddly comforting metafiction, like telling a child his tiny turtle has escaped out the window and gone to live in the lily pond on the golf course, when of course you found the poor thing shriveled up like an old apple core beneath the couch. Saying goodbye to Paul Walker may not be a milestone in cinematic history but it feels like the end of something important. Saying goodbye to Paul Walker means saying goodbye to innocence and heroism and guileless blue-eyed optimism. Saying goodbye to Paul Walker means saying goodbye to Saturday matinees and the magical intimacy of a family growing up together, to my sons as they come and go to college in Chicago and hiking trips in Montana, as they surge forth into their fast and furious American futures. Saying goodbye to Paul Walker means saying goodbye to everyone and everything I have ever loved. That turtle wasn't much, I suppose, but he meant a lot to some of us.

CRYPTOZOOLOGY

So long as kids still borrow the family car
to screw around joyriding
and tossing crushed beer cans out the windows
I shall feel at home in these United States.

Thank god for Henry Ford.
Thank god for Texas,

minus which our fabled republic
would resemble a box of jelly donuts
without no goddamn coffee.

Perhaps I'm naive
but if the Tasmanian wolf is still alive anywhere
it's in the wail of feedback and amp-garbled blues chords

of some insane teenage garage band, isn't it,
isn't it, I mean—isn't
it?

ANOTHER NIGHT AT LESTER'S

1.

Many of the voices I'm hearing these days
belong to actual people;
others resemble Ashbery poems recited by preschoolers.

Self-importance is something I learned from a self-help manual;
    pretentiousness I come by naturally.

My thanks to the generations yet to come
for their preorders of my *Collected Works*.

2.

In the next six hundred poems I'm going to read
tonight all words will be buzzwords,
all metaphors ink-edged, all images
pitched to tickle the funny bone and melt the heart
and vent some spleen
and pickle my liver and give you the finger.

3.

I had a thought and then I had a thought
and then I had another thought.

Check it out, the pics are on Instagram.

People who bought the items in your cart
also bought books about André Breton and Lindsay Lohan,
which tells you what, exactly?

4.

This has been a test of the Emergency Broadcast System.

Wrong button.

This has been an Audible audio text recording—
thank you for listening to Campbell McGrath's poem
"Another Night at Lester's,"
based on the novel *Push,* by Sapphire.

SLEEPWORK

I. MY HISTORY

Nothing much happens. And so we begin.
So we begin to negotiate the alphabet of regrets
and passions such chronicles are written in.
Begun and, already, done. So soon, so easily?
In the end the house falls down. And so do we.

II. READING LATE

Reading late, globed in shaded lamplight,
the family long asleep, the house restored
to its timbre of groaning night sounds,
a nocturne of peeping tree frogs, the soft moans
of palm fronds and termite-ridden beams.

III. SYNTAX

Deep, sensual pleasure of the book—
crack of a taut spine, allure of the page
and its must, its skitter, its ply—

life as it exists
there, as we exist in it,
reflections in a drop of mercury,

all the letters
of all the alphabets of every language
harnessed to meaning by syntax.

IV. A PAPER BOAT

At last I can be free and alone
and fold my news
into a paper boat I step into and set sail at once
to live my life inside a dream.

V. DREAM #1

He dreams that a giraffe is eating his toes, he dreams of emolument,
lucre, a jar of balm.

VI. DREAM #2

He dreams of espionage, a set of codes and tasks too complex to
understand, even in the dream it is clear how pointless it all is, and
he dismisses that dream, and moves on.

VII. SLEEPWORK

     Heart's calibration,
soul's equivocation,
     harmonic incandescence,
the proving of axioms,
     tightening the weave,
stacking bales,
     concourse with whales,
cavern travel
     lantern trimming,
ore refining,
     dream-mining.

VIII. WAKING

This is what I get paid for, he thinks—rising from bed to jot down
in his notebook the poem streaming like a ticker tape through his
dream—except for the part about getting paid.

IX. PROPAGANDA OF THE FRAGMENT

The recalcitrance of stars
in their medicinal bathwater, the ego

swaddled in power like the capsule
of the rocket borne on a pillar of flame,

narrative loosed within the text
like Cossacks upon the steppe.

The myth of junction is coterminous
with the dream of desired form,

a world in which parrots fly
into the wallpaper to complete its design.

Rivets replaced by carbon bonds,
women willowy as T'ang dynasty reeds,

trade wind carrying the sound of gunshots—
I'm awake now, I'm wide awake.

X. DREAM #3

He dreams of falling asleep, and waking up ravenous, and falling
asleep again, and wonders within the dream whether he really did
wake up, and if so, what he ate for breakfast.

XI. MY LIBRARY

Assembled with such care over the decades, with its shelves of well-thumbed *Collected Poems*, its ponderous chronicles, tea-stained chapbooks, and paperbacks asterisked with mildew, after all these years my library slips its anchor and sails ever more certainly into the past. Soon even the methods and substance of its origin—paper and ink, the printing press—will resemble fragments of ash and animal bone in an ancient digging, yet I feel no particular sense of regret that I will not live to see our futuristic tropes put to the final test, whatever dire exigency that might consist of. All I have ever wanted is to write a poem as ineradicable as the sun, singular as a wolf in its kingdom of moonlit ice. But who has time, anymore, for idle tasks? Why should anyone bother to adjudicate the petty crimes of language, border disputes between synonyms, lexical transgressions opaque as tax legislation? Pea vines are climbing the neighbor's trellis, the kids are looking for a surfboard behind the garage, wind rustles the branches which respond with shrugs and apologetic bows. In the shelter of their anthologies, the poems talk softly in the darkness, huddled together for warmth, waiting.

XII. DREAM #4

He has never seen the river he is dreaming but it is full of nuclear submarines and his kayak is full of holes.

XIII. LINES

front lines credit lines bread lines / lines of demarcation / blood lines punch lines / lines of broken glass / lines of trees in windrows across a far field / blue hills in broken lines on the horizon / blurred lines white lines / lines in the sand lines of questioning / life lines tag lines stat lines / lines of code / stress lines fracture lines fate

lines last lines / lines of birds flying south against the frost / lines of
golden tiles in an unfinished mosaic

XIV. JAPANESE EGGPLANT

What was learned in the garden is not a dream
but a tactile memory, a prickling in the fingertips
at the border between waking and sleep—
that the leaves of the Japanese eggplant
hide in their profusion a host of invisible thorns.

XV. DREAM #5

He tries to name the city he is dreaming and when he smells tahini
and poppy seeds he thinks, Atlantic Avenue, so this is Brooklyn.

XVI. A CONTINENT

Kids in Nebraska dreaming of volcanoes,
kids on the shore of Lake Managua
dreaming of jobs in shiny convenience stores—

go ahead, you can
walk there,
it's a continent.

XVII. HONEY

O, muse, wake me now from troubled dreams.
Take me one more time into your salt
and kelp-entangled arms before the storm arrives.
Make me greedy.
Make me sop up spilled honey with your crusts.

XVIII. DREAM #6

He dreams of the old Italian restaurant in Washington with Chianti
bottles covered in red wax, a jukebox of arias from *Aïda* and *Don
Giovanni,* the courtyard fountain of Poseidon in which he floated
boats made from corks and toothpicks with his brother, brackish
water alive with black eels served to favored customers, swish of
their tails below the surface like prehistoric creatures drowning in
tar, like the downstroke of a dozen bows as the violins commence
the second-movement adagio.

XIX. TERMITES

Look, the window of the dream is closing—
goodbye, monumental room
of snow globes and animal tusks.

Strip away the walls and what's left:
strakes and laths of old wood against plaster
oozing like stale frosting between them.

Let the termites take it all.

XX. MY JUSTICE

will not be found in a bullet
or a bottle
or the paper ark of any poem.

Hives can't hold enough bees
to pollinate all the wildflowers
watered by human tears.

The stone of your pain, no matter how tightly
you squeeze it, will never yield enough
to quench anybody's thirst.

Go on now, go back to bed,
get back to work,
return to the dream-swarm harvesting the nectar

of whatever it is you love enough
to have risked
this journey into darkness for.

THE RED DRAGONFLY: AFTER SHIKI

In Memory of David Dubrow, 1992–2013

1.

The red dragonfly
knows the way to the grave site—
one-year unveiling.

One-year unveiling,
out past the airport—*Tile Works,
Oasis Dream Spa.*

Sound of the airplanes
taking wing does not disturb
the red dragonfly.

Yellow butterfly,
late summer in Miami,
no sign of autumn.

No sign of autumn,
the greens and blues of summer
too bright for our eyes.

Too bright for our eyes,
the red dragonfly's shadow
falls on David's stone.

2.

The red dragonfly
watching, darting, hovering,
thinking of David.

Thinking of David—
honor the dead by living—
thinking of Shiki.

The mockingbird sings
all day without noticing
tears falling on stone.

Tears falling on stone
as butterflies flutter from
flower to flower.

Flower to flower,
hour to hour and day by day,
thinking of David.

The red dragonfly,
the yellow butterfly, the stone
bearing David's name.

3.

Little lizard, hide
from the mockingbirds with us,
summer's survivors.

Yellow butterfly,
honor the dead by living
like grass in sunshine.

Like grass in sunshine—
even by grief, mockingbird,
the soul is nourished.

Summer sun at noon,
and still autumn comes too soon,
even here, too soon.

Too bright for our eyes,
the greens and blues of summer,
tears falling on stone.

O, red dragonfly,
hover here, above his grave,
after we have gone.

FOUR ELEGIES

1. LYNDA HULL

What was the name of that bar beneath the El
in a neighborhood of matadors and jade-sequined fur?
Who dined with us in the district of thrashing eels
in bright blue buckets along cobblestones near a river
of sangria we could not for all our willingness drown
in or drink dry? Who taught the alchemical moon to ignite,
who spray-painted stars on the roof of the night?
Which room of the dream are you dying in now
that your hotel is filled with candy canes and broken glass?
Which horses, which alphabets, which strangers, which dawns?
Which triumph, which circle, which keyhole, which rhyme?
Avenues we swam through, a bride we traipsed past,
skeletons of syntax, a dagger, a mute swan.
Which room of the dream, Lynda, which room?

2. TOMAS TRANSTRÖMER

Clouds on the horizon, liturgical scrivening,
their shadows like ink stains on the sea.

Half a glass of wine, pale irises
declining to parchment,
rust which erupts
through the white paint of the lawn chairs

like a map

to the labyrinth of regret: that time passes,
that the kingdom of each instant
arises and vanishes, this is the essential,
the abiding enigma
of our existence, but not the only one.

How tedious to be born
into a world
with just one mystery.

3. C. K. WILLIAMS

His poetry arrives like a message in a bottle
from the Age of Reason,
the meditations of an Enlightenment polymath

with a Freudian grasp
of the ego
and its discontents

found on a beach somewhere along the coast
of an insular, self-satisfied nation
proud to be ignorant

of what lies beyond its shores, godless
monsters, marvelous beasts,
and other such tomfoolery. If only there was a way

to remove those poems
a man might
find some use for a bottle like that.

4. FRANZ WRIGHT

The moment, at dusk, after
the mirror shatters,
there is another moment
when
it assembles
the falling darkness
into a puzzle of the falling darkness,

and then it falls.

MY MOODS

My moods are many,
oh my many, many moods,

my fits, my jags, my blues,
my ahhs, my ohs, my oohs,

my highs and lows,
my downs and ups,
my under-the-mistletoes,
my in-his-cups,

my here and now,
my now and then,
my if not, why not,
my if-not-now-when,

my blood feuds, my sodality,
my lone-wolf ideology,
my birds-of-a-feather flock,
my steady-as-a-rock,
my swings and swerves,
my bundle of nerves,
my bliss, my blah, my glum, my glee,
my beck and call,
my call-and-response,
my Viennese waltz, my hoedown, my line dance,
my quicksand, my pedestal,
my saltwater crawl,
my acupuncture needle,
my thimble, my awl,
my Dremel, my ripsaw, my shock and awe,
my each and my any,
my silver dollar, my lucky penny,

my sickness and health,
my man and wife.

So there you are
at last, my dear,
ill as you are,
struggling for breath,
my compass rose, my one and only,
my shining star,
my life and death,

Elizabeth.

And all I feel is fear.

TOOLS

Wheels sigh with longing for the horizon.
Hunger moans in the spoon's hollow belly.
Tools recount the needs from which they arose
and so comprise a history of human desire.

The match recalls fear in the fireless night,
the saw's oiled teeth plead for perfect order,
the pen cannot imagine life without ink.

Even that technology employed by the soul
in its perilous escape from the prison of the body
is exhibited here, in these letters, in words.

WORDS

Messages dwell within words
like shadows inside dimly lit houses.
How did Rilke envision *Innerweltraum*?
What does Nietzsche mean by *will*?

No matter how we flood the night
darkness builds a nest beneath the eaves
and draws us inward. Otherwise
we might never have opened the door

or dug the foundation
or shaped the bricks to build the house,
abandoned now
to the immaculate webs of spiders.

TWO NOCTURNES

1.

He tries to sleep but the night is too complexly fraught, too many
echoes, too many absences, too much nothingness to relinquish
oneself to, elastic resistance of the void catapulting the mind back
toward the surface and marooning it there, rejection disguised
as rescue. In the living room the TV broadcasts mute images to
nobody, faces of the little space-alien cancer kids, saucer-eyed,
bald as cocoons, blinking their frail and elegant lashes like erotic
manga ghosts. Cool air in the window, sea grape leaves scattered
like desert islands across the courtyard and something tender
in the bottom of his foot, a thorn, encysted now, painful to the
touch.

A dusting of scent, barely discernible—not jasmine, not camellia—
late blossoms of the lemon tree.

Fog off the ocean painting the pine needles with salt.

Two chameleons beneath the porch light: they know that moths
will come if they wait, so they wait.

The limbs of the lemon tree, once bright with flowers, are heavy
with infant lemons, nuptial fruit amid the thorns.

Staring into the yard he remembers, for no good reason, a story
he heard the day before.

Someone had brought silver glitter to the birthday party. They
tossed it into the air on the pool deck and it was an exploding
blossom and then it was a scattering of ashes and then it was
everywhere, like grit, even the cake covered with it. Some worried

that it might be toxic, others hoped it might serve as an antitoxin against the loneliness circulating in their bloodstream.

Either way, it was a celebration: they had no choice but to eat.

2.

Transformation, disintegration, entropy, loss,
fragments of song

carried from hotels along the ocean on a wind tasting of oysters, pine resin, and brine.

Feldspar and mullein, sprigs of parsley, days of ether in a field of wild rye under Russian skies, imperial figurines carved from antique elephant ivory, wave-worn seashells and old scarred plastics—the marble-hard artificiality of bowling balls hurled so long the bowling alley has become a tavern, then a Laundromat, then a pawnshop in a section of the city once up-and-coming now spiraling inexplicably into terminal destitution or postindustrial malaise, no one seems sure which, no one wants to risk a guess, there is no one even to ask on that street of silvery northern sunlight, amid the gutter-collected leaves of autumn.

How do you know where any path will lead, which rock the salamander hides beneath?

Everything vanishes, but where does it go?

Here is the flower seller with her cart, the policeman chewing gum, the spotted puppy, bees at the gates of nectar, slender branches castigated by wind. You can smell the lingering fragrance of flowers from the lemon tree but you cannot touch them—where are they now, in which index or chronicle is that precise configuration of atomic vibrations recorded—when the boyish policeman greets the flower girl as a bumblebee alights on a bloodred chrysanthemum—that instant erased like steam from a mirror?

Not to resolve the conflicts, not to reconcile the narratives: set down the questions, side by side, and do not fear.

Before dawn the wind calms, the fog begins to lift.

Now the deep calculus of words surrounds him and he loses his way, as one awakening to find there is no door in the wall he stumbles against in the darkness, willing his dream to overmaster the reality of a long-familiar room.

MY ESTATE

The meanings I make inevitably make me.
As of chalk or apricots, of nouns and verbs.
The meanings I forsake cascade to the sea
in floods, in spasms. As the commonwealth of words

enfranchises its constituents in perpetuity,
so the interpreted world remains a diamond mine,
a cornucopia of semiotic superfluity.
Of gems, then. And stone fruit. And slant rhyme.

RELEASING THE SHERPAS

The last two sherpas were the strongest,
faithful companions, their faces wind-peeled,
streaked with soot and glacier-light on the snowfield
below the summit where we stopped to rest.

The first was my body, snug in its cap of lynx
fur, smelling of yak butter and fine mineral dirt,
agile, impetuous, broad-shouldered,
alive to the frozen bite of oxygen in the larynx.

The second was my intellect, dour and thirsty,
furrowing its fox-like brow, my calculating brain
searching for some cairn or chasm to explain
my decision to send them back without me.

Looking down from the next, axe-cleft serac
I saw them turn and dwindle and felt unafraid.
Blind as a diamond, sun-pure and rarefied,
whatever I was then, there was no turning back.

Part Two

Poems

THE HUMAN HEART

We construct it from tin and ambergris and clay,
    ochre, graph paper, a funnel
    of ghosts, whirlpool
in a downspout full of midsummer rain.

It is, for all its freedom and obstinance,
    an artifact of human agency
    in its maverick intricacy,
its chaos reflected in earthly circumstance,

its appetites mirrored by a hungry world
    like the lights of the casino
    in the coyote's eye. Old
as the odor of almonds in the hills around Solano,

filigreed and chancelled with flavor of blood oranges,
    fashioned from moonlight,
    yarn, nacre, cordite,
shaped and assembled valve by valve, flange by flange,

and finished with the carnal fire of interstellar dust.
    We build the human heart
    and lock it in its chest
and hope that what we have made can save us.

THE GOLDEN ANGEL PANCAKE HOUSE

Or coming out of Bento on a wild midwinter
midnight, or later, closing time Ron says, the last
rack of pool balls ratcheted down until dawn,
bottles corked and watered, lights out, going out
the door beneath the El tracks over Clark and Sheffield,
always a train showing up just then, loud, sure
as hell showering sparks upon the snowfall,
shaking slightly the lights and trestles, us
in our fellowship shouting and scurrying
like the more sprightly selves we once inhabited
behind parked cars and street signs, thinking,
hey, should we toss some snowballs? Bull's-eye,
the beauty of fresh snow in the hands, like rubbing
tree bark to catch that contact high direct
from the inexplicable source, unique however
often repeated, carried along on woolen thumbs
to the next absolutely necessary thing,
sloe gin fizzes to Green Mill jazz or the horror
of Jägermeister at the Ginger Man or
one of those German bars up around Irving Park
where a sup of the Weiss beer on tap is enough
to convince me to forswear my stake in any vision
of the afterlife you might care to construct, say
the one with the photo of the owner in his Nazi
uniform beside a pristine fjord, could be Norway,
1940? Whichever, we're hungry now, cast out
into the false dawn of snow-coiffed streetlights
embowed like bowl-cut adolescents or
Roman emperors sated on frost, thumbs up
or down to hash & eggs at Manny's
or the locally infamous Alps, then there's one
at which I never ate though it looked absolutely
irreplaceable, the Golden Angel Pancake House,

which is a poem by Rilke I've never read
though I've used its restroom, seen its dim
celestial figures like alien life-forms
in a goldfish bowl, tasted its lonely nectar
in every stack of silver dollar buttermilk flapjacks,
though the food, for all I know, is unutterably
awful, the way it resonates is what carries me
down the swirled chords of memory
toward the bottom of the frosted glass
aquarium of dreams, whatever that means, it's
what it meant to me coming home those nights
from the Lutheran College after teaching
the *Duino Elegies* to the daughters and sons
of Minnesota farmers, the footbridge over
the North Branch of the Chicago River, frozen
solid, eddies of whirling ionized powder
around my boots in the bone-cold subzero
that makes the lights in the windows of houses
so painfully beautiful—is it the longing
to get the hell inside or the tears the wind
inevitably summons forth? Homeward,
all the way down Lincoln Avenue's amazing
arabesques and ethnic configurations
of Korean babushkas and Croatian karaoke
that feeling set upon me like the overture to god
knows what dread disease, that cathartic, lustral,
yes, idiot laughter, threat of tears in the gullet,
Adam's apple stringing its yoyo to follow
the bouncing ball, as if boulevards of such purity
could countenance no science but eudaemonics,
hardly likely, as if this promethean eruption
were merely one of the more colorful dog-
and-pony acts of simple happiness, acrobatic

dromedaries or narcoleptic dancing bears,
but which I've come to see with perfect hindsight
was no less than the mighty strongman
joy himself bending bars of steel upon a tattooed
skull, so much nobler and more rapacious
than his country cousins, bliss, elation, glee,
a troupe of toothless, dipsomaniacal clowns,
multiform and variable as flurries from blizzards,
while joy is singular, present tense, predatory, priapic,
paradoxically composed of sorrow and terror
as ice is made of water, dense and pure,
darkly bejeweled, music rather than poetry,
preliterate, lapidary, dumb as an ox, cruel as youth,
magnificent and remorseless as Chicago in winter.

THE ORANGE

Gone to swim after walking the boys to school.
Overcast morning, midweek, off-season,
few souls to brave the warm, storm-tossed waves,
not wild but rough for this tranquil coast.

Swimming now. In rhythm, arm over arm,
let the ocean buoy the body and the legs work little,
wave overhead, crash and roll with it, breathe,
stretch and build, windmill, climb the foam. Breathe,

breathe. Traveling downwind I make good time
and spot the marker by which I know to halt
and forge my way ashore. Who am I
to question the current? Surely this is peace abiding.

Walking back along the beach I mark the signs of erosion,
bide the usual flotsam of sea grass and fan coral,
a float from somebody's fishing boat,
crusted with sponge and barnacles, and then I find

the orange. Single irradiant sphere on the sand,
tide-washed, glistening as if new born,
golden orb, miraculous ur-fruit,
in all that sweep of horizon the only point of color.

Cross-legged on my towel I let the juice course
and mingle with the film of salt on my lips
and the sand in my beard as I steadily peel and eat it.
Considering the ancient lineage of this fruit,

the long history of its dispersal around the globe
on currents of animal and human migration,

and in light of the importance of the citrus industry
to the state of Florida, I will not claim

it was the best and sweetest orange in the world,
though it was, o great salt water
of eternity,
o strange and bountiful orchard.

SUGAR OR BLOOD

In the kitchen Elizabeth has been making marmalade
with the luxurious crop of our lemon tree,
and from my desk I can almost taste the caramelizing essence
of citrus rind and vanilla beans and burnt sugar,
and I can hear the piano concerto by Mozart she is listening to,
which sounds like a pavilion constructed from lemon-tinted panes
    of sugar-glass,
and the Zairean music I'm listening to is like a tessellated and
    betasseled tapestry
thrown upon the floor of a nomad's tent, and the sands of the
    Sahara
continue their migration into the timeworn grasslands of the Sahel,
and the Virunga volcanoes comprise a fog-shouldered heaven
to the last families of mountain gorillas awaking before dawn,
shy, Herculean versions of ourselves, brothers
from a simpler dream, luminous and transient as meteors.
There will come no more into this world
when we have killed the last of them. So many
spools of golden sorrow to unwind,
so much pathos to weave upon a loom of human agency.
As if we were not ourselves baboons on the savannah,
not jackals, not giraffes in our ungainliness.
As if to desire the coat of a jaguar, the fur of a snow leopard,
was not a form of worship, as raw ore minted and coined
resembles the child's flattering imitation of a mastery it will never
    equal.
Who would not be a great cat in the Amazon or the Hindu Kush?
Even the greenish pelt of a river monkey, its iridescent aura,
even our too-human bodies shimmer with the weird, atomic eclipse-
    light of life.
Talking to myself like this, in a blazon and an emblem,
I realize I have never said plainly most of what I truly believe,
I have shied from difficulty and misstated my deepest fears,

I have not born full witness to the suffering in the streets of the
    cities I love,
I have not walked a picket line against the tyranny of greed,
I have been wily and evasive even on behalf of art,
I have not praised the movies in tones equal to the rapture
I have known there,
I cannot remember *King Lear,*
I did not finish *Ulysses* or even start on Proust,
even now I seek diversion in the candy necklace of delight,
even now I refuse to commit,
even now I would walk among jaguars
wearing the skin of a jaguar
as if it were not necessary to declare my allegiance,
as if I did not have to choose.
Which will it be, sugar or blood?

CAPITALIST POEM #5

I was at the 7-Eleven.
I ate a burrito.
I drank a Slurpee.
It was late, after work, washing dishes.
The burrito was good.
I had another.

I did it every day for a week.
I did it every day for a month.

To cook a burrito you tear off the plastic wrapper.
You push button #3 on the microwave.
Burritos are large, small, or medium.
Red or green chili peppers.
Beef or bean or both.
There are 7-Elevens all across the nation.

On the way out I bought a quart of beer for $1.39.
I was aware of social injustice

in only the vaguest possible way.

SUNRISE AND MOONFALL,
ROSARITO BEACH

What I remember of Mexico
is how the glass apple of mescal glowed
and exploded like a globe of seeds
or something we couldn't pronounce
or know the secret name of, never,
and even when the federales shook us down for twenty bucks,
as they must, to save face,
I couldn't lose the curve and rupture
of that sphere—half-full, hand-blown, imperfect
as our planet. Sure, everything is blowing open
now, all the freeways and skinheads, the music
invisibly blasting, radio waves invading the spines and craniums
of all this. San Diego, Tijuana, the Beach of Dead Dogs
where we slept in the cold, local kids incredulous
of Ed up early for no reason
driving golf balls out into the restlessly pounding surf.
Jesus, we're always hitting golf balls. It seems to be
some irreducible trait. There's Rob smashing the plaster icons,
all the bleeding martyrs and aqua pigs
and pink squinting Virgins the radiant chapel of candles
induced us to need. Jesus, let me ask, please,
before he decapitates you also with a wicked six-iron slice,
why are we always the ones on the beach
as dawn sucks the last drops from mescaline shards,
the ones who beat the sacred iguanas to death
as the sun comes right up
and the shadow-globe finally dances off stage,
the moon, I mean,
that other white world of men
driving golf balls to seas of dust and oblivion—
chrome-headed, flag-waving, violently American.

NIGHT TRAVELERS

Rising from Newark I see the cars of the homebound commuters
assembled like migrating caravans.
Lush as glowworms, gregarious as electric eels in their dusty blue
Hondas and plush Monte Carlos,
they jam the tollways and access roads, flood the exits and passing
lanes, circle the sinuous clover leaves
until they are nothing but rivers of dun and aluminum and butter-
colored light,
arterial channels of ivory and gold, pythons transmuting the
freeway web to luminous honeycomb.
Now I see the Trojan horses of industry, refineries and loading
docks at Elizabeth.
Now the magic kingdom itself, Manhattan, pathologically lucid on
Midsummer's eve,
which according to the book I'm trying to lose myself in as we
shudder to scale the oxygen stairwell
was the optimal hour for witches' transport by broomstick and
airborne bread paddle,
the dancing of mad hags under Venus Mountain, the Wild Hunt's
enchanted stampede,
covenants and covens, auguries and invocations, henbane,
belladonna, elderberry, hemlock,
as the travelers to Hackensack and Scotch Plains must suffer the
runes and rituals of unemancipated flight,
hubbed enumerations and the tokens of interchange, the ghosts of
evening loosed from backyard barbeques
as from the window I hear the song of baseball cards in bicycle
spokes and crickets in the neighbors' lawn,
lost summers of crabgrass, resin of oak leaves, taste of chalk from
the window screen
as I wait for the sound of my father's car in the driveway, Ford
Falcon, 1963,

as even now I imagine the children are sent to bed with patio voices
    and urn-light of fireflies in jelly-jar sarcophagi,
all the children in all the suburbs, tens of thousands, millions of
    them rising into the air in striped pajamas,
hovering like midget astronauts, tiny inmates in coonskin caps,
    convict stars above a nation of lawn chairs and tinkling ice cubes
and sprinklers whirling like tireless apostles, the beautiful sprinklers
    casting their nets, whispering silver apologies to the dust.
Now the air-nurse is passing out thimbles of whiskey, the pilot has
    spoken of vectors and altitude,
trajectory, velocity, how distance reduces to speed over time, the
    ways our lives reduce
to intervals of burnished light on the freeway, a ritual semaphore of
    stop-and-go traffic, sleepy kisses, radio static,
the invisible jet stream propelling us forward as the past recedes like
    farmland beneath our wings.
There are no spells against this grief, no incantations to bridge the
    longings of memory,
days and nights I cherish far better than projected wind speed or
    nomenclature of root salves.
I don't really know when midsummer falls or sign of nightshade or
    if the moon has risen at all beyond the acetylene clouds,
but I am rising to 31,000 feet and as far as I can see there is nothing
    but darkness
and nothing on this craft but bourbon and water and light the color
    of bourbon and water to ease the fire of our passage.

SLEEP

Falling asleep you do not traffic in abstractions:
you fashion images in the mind and count them.
You step back from the brink of thought,
from cognitive manipulation, to pure envisioning.
The sheep jump the wall, the skier parses new trails
on the mountain, swooping between spruce trees.
Elizabeth walks through homes she has known:
an old apartment in Chicago, our beloved hovel
on Jane Street, her childhood house in Baltimore.
What's down this hall, which door is the closet?
Turn on the light, examine the faded wallpaper,
move through the space, feel it, inhabit it.
What's been subtracted is a kind of pictorial syntax,
the filmic and interpretive operations of the mind
driving the images forward. Or, is that wrong?
You must remember to count the leaping sheep,
to engage the algebraic half of the mind,
which is the left or the right? Does it matter?
Two hemispheres, globe and brain,
night and day, the mad serendipity of it all.
What is the evolutionary purpose of sleep?
What is knowledge? Why are we alive?
Where is this world we find ourselves in?
How can we understand it? Who are we?

WHERE THE WATER RUNS DOWN

1

High Country Crags and Moon, Sunrise

In Ansel Adams's photograph the moon disintegrates
like sandstone. The inverted V of cliff in shadow
and the chevron of dark sky nearly meet
to consume the crest
of carefully delineated sunlight along the ridge.
This clarity signals a vision
without mitigation. It is a pure, chromatic world,
a landscape where ideas dominate facts
as light determines exposure.

Dry pines along her flanks. Douglas fir and juniper
remain hidden in the deeper arroyos.

In the next frame, *Aspens,*
Dawn, Dolores River Canyon
become wardens of an Emersonian ideal,
light thrown scintillant off edges and spires like needles
or a wave towing zones of sure and distinct tonality
down a slope of boulders and loose scree,
a tragic quality to the shadows of the transcendent grove,
until each white-fingered branch, each dew-glazed bud,
is lit from within.

2

Oregon state is mighty fine
if you're hooked on to the power line.

—WOODY GUTHRIE

What Woody Guthrie leaves out of his song
about the Grand Coulee Dam
is not the flumed bulk
shouldering clouds and mountains aside.
Neither is it the beauty of the black river;
the smell of horses in rain in the wild gorge country;
the catalogue of states gripped by dust and Depression—
Texas, Oklahoma, Kansas, Georgia, Tennessee;
nor even the old desire to tame the wilderness,
to shape river and mountain and desert to man's will.
What's never mentioned, left unsung,
is the nature of that time
when a dam was something to sing about—
an attitude of profound wonder, honed by despair,
humming through high-tension wires
all across the country,
technology's promise
brought to every town and ranch and farm—not only
along the sinuous Columbia choked with logs,
but everywhere, all over this land, from California
to the New York island. An era
finding voice in a song about *e-leca-tri-cy-tee.*
A vast, implicit history, east and west,
growth and opportunity and inequality,
crystalline in the moment—
just as a hologram, when shattered, retains

the image of the whole in every shard and fragment—
from Maine to Oregon,
from Plymouth Rock to the Grand Coulee Dam
where the water runs down.

3

                        What Ansel Adams leaves out
is neither song, stone, nor innuendo
of light cascading through rain-laced aspens.
Lost at the base of Blanca Peak
are two figures: one pulls up stakes
while the other stirs a pot of coffee with a tin spoon.
They hike all day along the ridgeline
and at evening make camp in a valley
where a thin stream is marked by alder
and gooseberries. They build a fire
to cook macaroni and cheese, and heat cans of beans
in the coals for dinner. Late at night,
in contrast to all rules of composition,
they beat a riven, smoldering log with pine boughs
sending sparks like clouds and flocks of birds
and winter storm in the valley
rising up to the stars, splinters of light or stone,
innumerable and inseparable.

BOOKS

Books live in the mind like honey inside a beehive,
that ambrosial archive, each volume sealed in craft-made paper,
nutritive cells, stamen-fragrant, snug as apothecary jars.

Like fossilized trilobites, or skulls in a torchlit catacomb
beneath an ancient city, Byzantium or Ecbatana,
or Paris at the end of April when vendors set their folding tables
filled with lily-of-the-valley beside every Métro entrance,

and the women, coming home from work or market,
scented already with the fugitive perfume of *muguets,*
carry handheld bouquets like pale tapers
through the radiant, rain-washed streets at sunset.

And then it is night, half the world ruled by dreams
from which arise narrative forms—riddles, fables, myths—
as mist lifts from mountain valleys in autumn,
as steam belches from fumaroles in benthic trenches

to whose sulfuric cones strange life-forms cling,
chrome-green crabs and eyeless shrimp, soft-legged starfish
sung to sleep by that curious cousin of the hippopotamus,

the whale, who, having first evolved from ocean to land
in the ever-eventful Cretaceous, thought better of it,
returning, after millions of years, to scholarly contemplation
in the mesomorphic, metaphysical library of the sea.

LATE SPRING

The kingdom of perception is pure emptiness.

—PO CHÜ-I

1.

I have faltered in my given duty.
It is a small sacrilege, a minor heresy.

The nature of the duty is close attention
to the ivy and its tracery on riled brick,

the buckled sidewalk, the optimistic fern,
downed lilacs brown as coffee grounds,

little twirled seedwings falling by the thousands
from the maples in May wind,

and the leaves themselves
daily greener in ripening sunlight.

To whom is their offering rendered,
and from whom derived,

these fallen things
urging their bodies upon the pavement?

There is a true name for them,
a proper term, but what is it?

2.

Casting about, lachrymose, the branches
of the trees at 4 A.M.

flush with upthrust flowers,
like white candles in blackened sconces.

All day I was admonished
to admire the beauty of this single peony

but only now, in late starlight,
do I crush its petals to my face.

Elemental silk dimmed to ash,
reddening already to the brushstroke of dawn,

its fragrance is a tendril
connecting my mind to the rain,

a root, a tap, a tether.
Such is the form of the duty,

but which is its officer,
the world or the senses?

The many languages of birds now,
refusing to reconcile,

and clouds streaming out of the darkness
like ants to the day's bound blossom.

SPICER

Then sadness came upon them. Memories of love
or sorrow, favorite cats, barnyard animals,
dirt where called for
and all the appropriate longings, lusts, self-pity,
even rage at some tyrannical lapse of manners
over Chinese food—just so each chosen beam or ray,
each this, each that, so special and unique:
Grandma's ribbon of Kansas whalebone,
hedge clippers from the root cellar
of the dazed horticulturist. Time passes. The years
groove one by one round the garlanded Maypole,
and the presence of natural totems
bears a significant impact on the order of our lives,
dew-struck daylilies dieseling skyward,
the beauty of the crab apple tree against a derelict wall,
each fruit a form of grace or an admission
of human frailty. *You're the MSG in my shark's fin soup,*
but I yam what I yam, sweet potato.
The rage of our days rises like lobster claws
doused in fake butter
from a seafood restaurant chain,
but in the end, dancing, we unfasten
our rainbow suspenders and lie down with death,
mongrel death, gym coach death
tossing dodgeballs of extirpation, turning somersaults
of grief on misery's wrestling mats. Everything passes,
rain dissolving a lost box of cough drops, so many
Dutch Apple Pop-Tarts in the heart's toaster oven.
Things are like that. We're like that,
alone together, ignorant of shadows as cardamom
or star anise reveling in sunlight,
wild seeds blind to the spicer's approach.

INVITATIONS

To rhetoric: quarry me
for the stones of such tombs as may rise
in your honor.

To molecules: let me be carbon.
To the burners of bones: let me be charcoal.

To the drosophila: declaim to me
of finger bananas.

To eyes: that they might look askance
in the darkness and find me.

EMILY AND WALT

I suppose we did not want for love.
They were considerate parents, if a bit aloof,

or more than a bit. He was a colossus
of enthusiasms, none of them us,

while she kissed our heads and mended socks
with a wistful, faraway look.

She might have been a little, well, daft.
And he—*Allons, my little ones*, he'd laugh,

then leave without us.
And those "friends" of his!

Anyway, he's gone off to "discover
himself" in San Francisco, or wherever,

while she's retired to the condo in Boca.
We worry, but she says she likes it in Florida;

she seems, almost, happy. I suppose they were
less caregivers than enablers,

they taught by example, reading for hours
in the drafty house and now the house is ours,

with its drawers full of junk and odd
lines of verse and stairs that ascend to god

knows where, belfries and gymnasia,
the chapel, the workshop, aviaries, atria—

we could never hope to fill it all.
Our voices are too small

for its silences, too thin to spawn an echo.
Sometimes, even now, when the night wind blows

into the chimney flue
I start from my bed, calling out—"Hello,

Mom and Dad, is that you?"

FLORIDA

There is no hope of victory in this garden.
Bent to the lawn, I acknowledge defeat
in every blade of St. Augustine
grass destroyed by intractable chinch bugs.

Hours on end I pull the woody roots
of dollar weed from the soil. At night I dream
of vegetable genocide, so deep, so abiding,
has my hatred for that kingdom grown.

Near dawn I hear the scuttle of fruit rats
returning to their nest within our wall;
they walk the tightrope of the phone wires at dusk,
leap like acrobats into limbs of heavy citrus.

Something larger inhabits the crawl space,
raccoon or opossum, purple carapace
of the land crab emerging from its burrow.
On a branch, green caterpillars thick as a finger,

from which will rise some terrible night moth.
The snails leave calcified notice of their trespass;
in the rain they climb the hibiscus and wait.
I labor in sunlight, praying for stalemate.

CALIFORNIA LOVE SONG

To ride the Ferris wheel on a winter night in Santa Monica,
playing nostalgic songs on a Marine harmonica,
thinking about the past, thinking about everything
Los Angeles has ever meant to me, is that too much to ask?

To kiss on the calliope and uproot world tyranny
and strum a rhythm guitar Ron Wood would envy,
to long for the lost, to love what lasts, to sing
idolatrous praises to the stars, is that too much to ask?

Arm in arm to gallivant, to lark, to crow, to bask
in a wigwam of circus-colored atomic smog,
to quaff a plastic cup of nepenthean eggnog
over one more round of boardwalk Skee-Ball,
to trade my ocean for a waterfall,
to live with you or not at all, is that too much to ask?

ANGELS AND THE BARS
OF MANHATTAN

for Bruce Craven

What I miss most about the city are the angels
and the bars of Manhattan: faithful Cannon's and the Night Cafe;
the Corner Bistro and the infamous White Horse;
McKenna's maniacal hockey fans; the waitresses at Live Bait;
lounges and taverns, taps and pubs;
joints, dives, spots, clubs; all the Blarney
Stones and Roses full of Irish boozers eating brisket
stacked on kaiser rolls with frothing mugs of Ballantine.
How many nights we marked the stations of that cross,
axial or transverse, uptown or down to the East Village
where there's two in every block we'd stop to check,
hoisting McSorley's, shooting tequila and eight-ball
with hipsters and bikers and crazy Ukrainians,
all the black-clad chicks lined up like vodka bottles on Avenue B,
because we liked to drink and talk and argue,
and then at four or five when the whiskey soured
we'd walk the streets for breakfast at some diner,
Daisy's, the Olympia, La Perla del Sur,
deciphering the avenues' hazy lexicon over coffee and eggs,
snow beginning to fall, steam on the windows blurring the film
until the trussed-up sidewalk Christmas trees
resembled something out of Mandelstam,
Russian soldiers bundled in their greatcoats,
honor guard for the republic of salt. Those were the days
of revolutionary zeal. Haughty as dictators, we railed
against the formal elite, certain as Moses or Roger Williams
of our errand into the wilderness. Truly,
there was something almost noble
in the depth of our self-satisfaction, young poets in New York,
how cool. Possessors of absolute knowledge,
we willingly shared it in unmetered verse,

scavenging inspiration from Whitman and history and Hüsker Dü,
from the very bums and benches of Broadway,
precisely the way that the homeless
who lived in the Parks Department garage at 79th Street
jacked into the fixtures to run their appliances
off the city's live current. Volt pirates,
electrical vampires. But what I can't fully fathom
is the nature of the muse that drew us to begin with,
bound us over to those tenements of rage
as surely as the fractured words scrawled across the stoops
and shuttered windows. Whatever compelled us
to suspend the body of our dreams from poetry's slender reed
when any electric guitar would do? Who did we think was listening?
Who, as we cried out, as we shook, rattled, and rolled,
would ever hear us among the blue multitudes of Christmas lights
strung as celestial hierarchies from the ceiling? Who
among the analphabetical ranks and orders
of warped records and secondhand books on our shelves,
the quarterlies and *Silver Surfer* comics, velvet Elvises,
candles burned in homage to *Las Siete Potencias Africanas*
as we sat basking in the half-blue glimmer,
tossing the torn foam basketball nigh the invisible hoop,
listening in our pitiless way to two kinds of music,
loud and louder, anarchy and roar, rock and roll
buckling the fundament with pure, delirious noise.
It welled up in us, huge as snowflakes, as manifold,
the way ice devours the reservoir in Central Park.
Like angels or the Silver Surfer we thought we could
kick free of the stars to steer by dead reckoning.
But whose stars were they? And whose angels
if not Rilke's, or Milton's, even Abraham Lincoln's,
"the better angels of our nature" he hoped would emerge,
air-swimmers descending in apple-green light.

We worshipped the anonymous neon apostles of the city,
cuchifrito cherubs, polystyrene seraphim,
thrones and dominions of linoleum and asphalt:
abandoned barges on the Hudson mudflats;
Bowery jukes oozing sepia and plum-colored light;
headless dolls and eviscerated teddy bears
chained to the grilles of a thousand garbage trucks; the elms
that bear the wailing skins of plastic bags in their arms all winter,
throttled and grotesque, so that we sometimes wondered
walking Riverside Drive in February or March
why not just put up cement trees with plastic leaves
and get it over with? There was no limit to our capacity for awe
at the city's miraculous icons and instances,
the frenzied cacophony, the democratic whirlwind.
Drunk on thunder, we believed in vision
and the convocation of heavenly presences summoned
to the chorus. Are they with us still? Are they
listening? Spirit of the tiny lights, ghost beneath the words,
numinous and blue, inhaler of bourbon fumes and errant shots,
are you there? I don't know. Somehow I doubt we'll ever know
which song was ours and which the siren
call of the city. More and more, it seems our errand
is to face the music, bring the noise, scour the rocks
to salvage grace notes and fragmented harmonies,
diving for pearls in the beautiful ruins,
walking all night through the pigeon-haunted streets
as fresh snow softly fills the imprint of our steps.
OK, I'm repeating myself, forgive me, I'm sure brevity
is a virtue. It's just this melody keeps begging to be hummed:
McCarthy's, on 14th Street, where the regulars drink
beer on the rocks and the TV shows *Police Woman*
twenty-four hours a day; the quiet, almost tender way
they let the local derelicts in to sleep it off

in the back booths of the Blue & Gold after closing;
and that sign behind the bar at the Marlin, you know
the one, hand-lettered, scribbled with slogans of love and abuse,
shopworn but still bearing its indomitable message
to the thirsty, smoke-fingered, mood-enhanced masses—
"Ice Cold Six Packs To Go." Now that's a poem.

ODE TO A CAN OF SCHAEFER BEER

We would like to
express sincere
thanks to our
Schaefer customers
for their loyalty
and support.

It is brewed in Milwaukee, Wisconsin.
It knows its place.
It wears its heart on its sleeve
like a poem,
laid out like a poem
with weak line endings and questionable
closure. Its idiom
would not be unfamiliar
to a Soviet film director,
its emblem a stylized stalk
of bronzed wheat,
circlets of flowering hops
as sketched by a WPA draftsman
for a post office mural in 1934.
It conjures a forgotten social contract
between consumers and producers,
a world of feudal fealty—
the corporation
is your friend, your loyalty
shall be rewarded—a vision
of benign paternalism
last seen in *Father Knows Best*
and agitprop depictions of Mao
sharing party wisdom with eager villagers,
bestowing avuncular unction.

It was, once, *the one*
beer to have
when you're having more than one,
slogan and message
outdated as giant ground sloths roaming
the forests of Nebraska,
irrecoverable
as the ex-cheerleader
watching her toddler eat handfuls of sand
at the playground
considers that lost world of pompoms
and rah-rah-let's-go-team
to be.

It has earned no lasting portion of glory.
It has eaten crow
and humble pie. Long before it was faded
by the sun it appeared
faded by the sun, gathering dust
in the corner
of the bodega or the county store,
cylindrical, handy, holsterable,
its modesty honestly
come by, possessing the courage
of its simple convictions
like the unsuspected gunfighter
emerging from shadow
to defend the weak from tyranny.

And if we have moved forward,
unmasking the designs of the regime
upon our fertile valley,

learning to litigate against the evil sheriff,
such knowledge has left a bitter taste
in our mouths,
and if this can of beer
deserves our attention
it is as a reminder of what it meant
to speak without hypocrisy,
to live unironically,
to be sincere.

Thin, rice-sweet, tasting of metal
and crisp water,
it is no worse than many,
and if it is not an elixir it might serve
as an occasional draft
of refreshment and self-knowledge.

It was established in the United States in 1842.
It contains 12 fl. oz.

Store in a cool place
and drink responsibly.

POETRY AND THE WORLD

In the world of some poets
there are no Cheerios or Pop-Tarts, no hot dogs
tumbling purgatorially on greasy rollers,
only chestnuts and pomegranates,
the smell of freshly baked bread,
summer vegetables in red wine, simmering.

In the world of some poets
lucid stars illumine lovers
waltzing with long-necked swans in fields
flush with wildflowers and waving grasses,

there are no windowless classrooms,
no bare, dangling bulbs,
no anxious corridors of fluorescent tubes.

In the world of some poets
there is no money and no need
to earn it, no health insurance,
no green cards, no unceremonious toil.

And how can we believe in that world
when the man who must clean up after the reading
waits impatiently outside the door
in his putty-colored service uniform,
and the cubes of cheese at the reception
taste like ashes licked from a bicycle chain,
when the desktops and mostly empty seats
have been inscribed with gutter syllabics
by ballpoint pens gripped tight as chisels,
and the few remaining students are green
as convalescents narcotized by apathy?

But—that's alright. Poetry
can handle it.

Poetry is a capacious vessel, with no limits
to its plasticity, no end to the thoughts and feelings
it can accommodate,
no restrictions upon the imaginings
it can bend through language into being.

Poetry is not the world.
We cannot breathe its atmosphere,
we cannot live there, but we can visit,
like sponge divers in bulbous copper helmets
come to claim some small portion
of the miraculous.

And when we leave we must remember
not to surface too rapidly,
to turn off the lights in the auditorium
and lock the office door—there have been thefts
at the university in recent weeks.

We must remember not to take the bridge
still under construction, always under construction,

to stop on the causeway for gas

and pick up a pack of gum at the register,
and a bottle of water,
and a little sack of plantain chips,

their salt a kind of poem, driving home.

GIRL WITH BLUE PLASTIC RADIO

The first song I ever heard was "The Ballad of Bonnie and Clyde."
There was a girl at the playground with a portable radio,
lying in the grass near the swing set, beyond the sun-lustred
    aluminum slide,

kicking her bare feet in the air, her painted toenails—toes
the color of blueberries, rug burns, yellow pencils, Grecian urns.
This would be when—1966? No, later, '67 or '68. And no,

it was not the very first song I ever heard,
but the first that invaded my consciousness in that elastically joyous
way music does, the first whose lyrics I tried to learn,

my first communication from the gigawatt voice
of the culture—popular culture, mass culture, our culture—
    kaboom!—
raw voltage embraced for the sheer thrill of getting juiced.

Who wrote that song? When was it recorded, and by whom?
Melody lost in the database of the decades
but still playing somewhere in the mainframe cerebellums

of its dandelion-chained, banana-bike-riding, Kool-Aid-
addled listeners, still echoing within the flesh and blood mausoleums
of us, me, we, them, the selfsame blades

of wind-sown crabgrass spoken of and to by Whitman,
and who could believe it would still matter
decades or centuries later, in a new millennium,

matter what we listened to, what we ate and watched, matter
that it was "rock 'n' roll," for so we knew to call it,
matter that there were hit songs, girls, TVs, fallout shelters.

Who was she, her with the embroidered blue jeans and bare feet,
toenails gilded with cryptic bursts of color?
She is archetypal, pure form, but no less believable for that.

Her chords still resonate, her artifacts have endured
so little changed as to need no archeological translation.
She was older than me, worldly and self-assured.

She was, already, a figure of erotic fascination.
She knew the words and sang the choruses
and I ran over from the sandbox to listen

to a world she cradled in one hand, transistorized oracle,
blue plastic embodiment of our neo–Space Age ethos.
The hulls of our Apollonian rocket ships were as yet unbarnacled

and we still found box turtles in the tall weeds and mossy grass
by the little creek not yet become what it was all becoming
in the wake of the yellow earthmovers, that is:

suburbia. Alive, vibrant, unself-consciously evolving,
something new beneath the nuclear sun, something new in the
      acorn-scented dark.
Lived there until I was seven in a cinder-block garden

apartment. My prefab haven, my little duplex ark.
And the name of our subdivision was
Americana Park.

WHEEL OF FIRE, THE MOJAVE

What is this white intensity
swallowing me as the night swallows and now disgorges
only Jonah was rocked and the night
is sorrowful music
but this is something else? What is this absence,
immersion as faith is a kind of immersion,
a thirst for light in the true air?
Look at the sun's jailbreak over the violent
walls. I've driven all night
to find myself here. Look at the gypsum desert,
elements scattered like 7-Elevens all the way to Death Valley,
the way L.A. reaches into it, one hundred miles or more.

I'm talking about America, the thing itself,
white line unreeling, pure distance, pure speed.

I've driven all night

from fear of the darkness that would seize me if I stopped,
even coffee at a truck stop, even water. Look

at the wraiths of stars,
Buick Electras rusting in the freight meadow.

It is the ghost of the light that moves me.

I'm talking about the half-seen,
dawn and evening, desert orchids,
coyotes coming down to the river to drink.
I'm talking about the thing itself,
what rises in the night like anger or grief,
language-less, blistering and overbrimming

as a river coming down from the mountains
to die in the sinks of rushes and alkali,
the absolute purity of light or intention,
memory of grace, seagulls canting windward
above the Great Salt Lake—
                                    the sun, the desert,
the weight of the light is staggering—

until even the flesh of our days falls away,
ash from a cone, fruit from a stone. Even now

when the whirling miraculous
wheel in the sky has risen and vanished at first light,
gears of a huge engine, starlings
drunk on oxygen—
                            when the wheel
is gone and I am alone with the willows
at the edge of the utterly desolate
Mojave River.

                    I've driven all night toward the basin
of angels. I've driven all night without understanding

anything, need or desire, this desert, neon
signs remorseless as beacons.
                                    I'm talking about America.

I'm talking about loneliness, the thing itself.

I've driven all night to find myself

here. Look around you,
even now look around you.

Dawn breaking open the days like jeweled eggs,
Joshua trees crippled by this freakish rain of light.

CONSCIOUSNESS

An obsessive compulsion, a ring of keys,
a sequence of numerals to roll the tumblers
and open the golden vault, a web, a blizzard,
a stochastic equation to generate song.
It goes on. There is no satiety mechanism
in the market system, in the agora of thought.
We cannot bloom, cannot flower,
cannot crystallize into coal or diamond
or disassemble ourselves into pure melody.
Alone in the ruined observatory we stand
surrounded by astral bodies, glittering
milk-folds of star creation we stutter to name
but still we cannot burn our fingerprints
into the void. Into. The. Saints of it, myths of it,
cloister, waterwheel, winged lion, myrrh.
Knots of olive wood in a beached rowboat
over which to roast the tiny silver fish
delicious with salt and lemon. Marooned, then,
but well fed on the substance of this world.
And still forsaken. And still hungry.

SMOKESTACKS, CHICAGO

To burn, to smolder with the jeweled incendiary coal
of wanting, to move and never
stop, to seize, to use,
to shape, grasp, glut, these united
states of transition, that's
it, that is it,
our greatness, right
there. Dig down the ranges, carve out
rivers and handguns and dumps, trash it,
raze it, torch
the whole stuck-pig of it. Why
the fuck not? Immediately I am flying
past some probably
pickup truck with undeniable motor
boat in tow, a caravan
of fishermen no less, bass and bronze eucalyptus scars,
red teeth of erosion click-clacking
their bitterness. And
the sports fans
coming home through a rain
of tattered pompoms. And the restless
guns of suburban hunters shooting
skeet along the lake. Desire is
the name of every vessel out there, but
I think the wind that drives them
is darker. I think I see
the tiny sails are full of hate
and I am
strangely glad. Don't stop,
hate and learn to love your hatred,
learn to kill and love the killing of what you hate,
keep moving,
rage, burn, immolate. Let the one

great hunger flower
among the honeysuckle skulls
and spent shells
of the city. Let longing
fuel the avenues of bowling alleys and flamingo
tattoos. Let sorrow glean the shards
of the soul's bright jars
and abandoned
congregations. Harvest moon
above the petrified
forest of smokestacks.

THE BURNING SHIP

No room for regret or self-doubt in art,
doubt but not self-doubt. The ship hauls anchor,
the kerosene lantern flickers and goes out,
voices in the pitch black swell with anger

as shipmates mistake each other for enemies.
The lantern spills, the pilot drops a lit cigar.
Tragedy ensues and engenders more tragedy.
If only the moon could see, if only the stars

had been granted the power of speech.
But the blind remain blind, the voiceless mute.
The burning ship threads its way between reefs
in the darkness. Doubt, but not self-doubt.

THE FUTURE

I would speak to it as to a stream in the forest
where infant ferns grow shapely as serpents or violins.

I would surrender to it if I could drift among the stars
as among a cloud of milkweed spores, or jellyfish.

Years turn, like autumn leaves; they pass,
and we number them, like galaxies or symphonies,
when we should honor them with names,
like hurricanes, or the craters of the moon.

What will Arcturus ever mean to me
compared to these years—1962, 1986, 2005?

They march beside me like siblings,
they are more intimate than lovers,
they do not turn back when I fall behind.

The future watches us and marvels
at our inability to comprehend it.

Even Einstein only glimpsed its shores,
like Magellan, planting small vineyards
at the edge of the ice, like Erik the Red.

To view it plainly we would need to evict
the self from its rough settlement,
to strip the bark from our limbs and branches,
to reside in a place where atoms and stars
resemble shy animals learning to eat from our hand.

Only then would the future, like a lonely hermit,
find its way to that clearing by the stream in the forest,
and sit beside us on a mossy stone, and listen.

THE ZEBRA LONGWING

Forty years I've waited,
uncomprehending,
for these winter nights
when the butterflies
fold themselves like paper cranes
to sleep in the dangling
roots of the orchids
boxed and hung
from the live oak tree.
How many there are.
Six. Eight. Eleven.
When I mist the spikes
and blossoms by moonlight
they stir but do not wake,
antennaed and dreaming
of passionflower
nectar. Never before
have they gifted us
in like manner, never before
have they stilled their flight
in our garden. Wings
have borne them away
from the silk
of the past as surely
as some merciful wind
has delivered us
to an anchorage of such
abundant grace,
Elizabeth. All my life
I have searched, without knowing it,
for this moment.

NIGHTS ON PLANET EARTH

Heaven was originally precisely that: the starry sky, dating back to the earliest Egyptian texts, which include magic spells that enable the soul to be sewn in the body of the great mother, Nut, literally "night," like the seed of a plant, which is also a jewel and a star. The Greek Elysian Fields derive from the same celestial topography: the Egyptian "Field of Rushes," the eastern stars at dawn where the soul goes to be purified. That there is another, mirror world, a world of light, and that this world is simply the sky—and a step further, the breath of the sky, the weather, the very air—is a formative belief of great antiquity that has continued to the present day with the godhead becoming brightness itself: *dios/theos* (Greek); *deus/divine/Diana* (Latin); *devas* (Sanskrit); *daha* (Arabic); *day* (English).

—SUSAN BRIND MORROW, *WOLVES AND HONEY*

1.

Gravel paths on hillsides amid moon-drawn vineyards,
click of pearls upon a polished nightstand
soft as rainwater, self-minded stars, oboe music
distant as the grinding of icebergs against the hull
of the self and the soul in the darkness
chanting to the ecstatic chance of existence.
Deep is the water and long is the moonlight
inscribing addresses in quicksilver ink,
building the staircase a lover forever pauses upon.
Deep is the darkness and long is the night,
solid the water and liquid the light. How strange
that they arrive at all, nights on planet earth.

2.

Sometimes, not often but repeatedly, the past invades my dreams in
   the form of a familiar neighborhood I can no longer locate,
a warren of streets lined with dark cafes and unforgettable bars, a
   place where I can sing by heart every song on every jukebox,
a city that feels the way the skin of an octopus looks pulse-changing
   from color to color, laminar and fluid and electric,
a city of shadow-draped churches, of buses on dim avenues, or
   riverlights, or canyonlands, but always a city, and wonderful,
   and lost.
Sometimes it resembles Amsterdam, students from the ballet school
   like fanciful gazelles shooting pool in pink tights and soft,
   shapeless sweaters,
or Madrid at 4 A.M., arguing *The Eighteenth Brumaire* with angry
   Marxists, or Manhattan when the snowfall crowns every trash
   can king of its Bowery stoop,
or Chicago, or Dublin, or some ideal city of the imagination, as in a
   movie you can neither remember entirely nor completely forget,
barracuda-faced men drinking sake like yakuza in a Murakami
   novel, women sipping champagne or arrack, the rattle of beaded
   curtains in the back,
the necklaces of Christmas lights reflected in raindrops on
   windows, the taste of peanuts and their shells crushed to
   powder underfoot,
always real, always elusive, always a city, and wonderful, and lost. All
   night I wander alone, searching in vain for the irretrievable.

3.

In the night I will drink from a cup of ashes and yellow paint.
In the night I will gossip with the clouds and grow strong.
In the night I will cross rooftops to watch the sea tremble in a
    dream.
In the night I will assemble my army of golden carpenter ants.
In the night I will walk the towpath among satellites and cosmic
    dust.
In the night I will cry to the roots of potted plants in empty offices.
In the night I will gather the feathers of pigeons in a honey jar.
In the night I will become an infant before your flag.

Part Three

Prose Poems

SUNSET, ROUTE 90,
BREWSTER COUNTY, TEXAS

Now the light is brass and pewter, alloyed metals solid as amber,
allied with water, umber and charnel, lucent as mercury, fugitive
silver, chalk-rose and coal-blue, true, full of the skulls and skeletons
of moon light, ash light and furnace light, West Texas whiskey light,
bevel light, cusp light, light fall of arches and architectonics, earth
light and anchor light, sermon light, gospel light, light that clasps
hands with the few and the many, mesa light, saltbush and longhorn
light, barbed wire and freight train light, light of the suffering,
light of the dusk-fallen, weal light and solace light, graveyard at the
crossroads light, flood light, harbor light, light of the windmills and
light of the hills, light that starts the dove from the thistle, light that
leads the horses to water, light of the boon and bounty of the Pecos,
light of the Christ of Alpine, light of the savior of Marathon, Jesus of
cottonwood, Jesus of oil, Jesus of jackrabbits, Jesus of quail, Jesus of
creosote, Jesus of slate, Jesus of solitude, Jesus of grace.

PLUMS

I'm sitting on a hill in Nebraska, in morning sunlight, looking
out across the valley of the Platte River. My car is parked far
below, in the lot behind the rest stop wigwam, beyond which runs
the highway. Beyond the highway: stitch-marks of the railroad;
the sandy channels and bars of the Platte, a slow wide bend of
cottonwood saplings metallic in the sun; beyond the river a hazy,
Cézanne-like geometry of earthy blues, greens, and browns fading,
at last, into the distance. Barrel music rises up from the traffic on
I-80, strings of long-haul truckers rolling west, rolling east, the
great age of the automobile burning down before my eyes, a thing
of colossal beauty and thoughtlessness. For lunch, in a paper bag:
three ripe plums and a cold piece of chicken. It is not yet noon. My
senses are alive to the warmth of the sun, the smell of the blood of
the grass, the euphoria of the journey, the taste of fruit, fresh plums,
succulent and juicy, especially the plums.

So much depends upon the image: chickens, asphodel, a numeral, a
seashell;

one white peony flanged with crimson;

a chunk of black ore carried up from the heart of anthracite to
be found by a child alongside the tracks like the token vestige
of a former life—what is it? *coal*—a touchstone polished by age
and handling, so familiar as to be a kind of fetish, a rabbit's foot
worn down to bone, a talisman possessed of an entirely personal,
associative, magical significance.

Why do I still carry it, that moment in Nebraska?

Was it the first time I'd been west, first time driving across the country? Was it the promise of open space, the joy of setting out, the unmistakable goodness of the land and the people, the first hint of connection with the deep wagon ruts of the dream, the living tissue through which the valley of the Platte has channeled the Mormons and the '49ers, the Pawnee and the Union Pacific, this ribbon of highway beneath a sky alive with the smoke of our transit, the body of the past consumed by the engine of our perpetual restlessness? How am I to choose among these things? Who am I to speak for that younger vision of myself, atop a hill in Nebraska, bathed in morning light? I was there. I bore witness to that moment. I heard it pass, touched it, tasted its mysterious essence. I bear it with me even now, an amulet smooth as a fleshless fruit stone.

Plums.

I have stolen your image, William Carlos Williams. Forgive me. They were delicious, so sweet and so cold.

RIFLE, COLORADO

I doubt they were used to strangers in the Rifle Cafe, wrapping
their sausage in pancakes a little after dawn. I think the earnest
woman frying eggs and the girl in the cowboy hat tracing her finger
through spilled flour were mother and daughter. I doubt the lined
man drinking bourbon at the bar was either father or brother. I
don't know where the guides would lead their parties to hunt for
bighorn and whitetail that day. I don't know how often they came to
the cafe, or what they thought about, or what they ate. I don't know
what their names were, where they lived, whether their families
raised cattle or horses or stayed in bed in the morning.

I do know that there were cowboy hats and dirty orange workmen's
gloves, the coffee was strong, the pancakes were good, Main Street
was gravel, the river ran by, the sun rose just as we got there,
night left the Rockies reluctantly, snow and timber diminished in
daylight, the mountains emerged slowly with dawn—high country
in winter is beautiful and lonely.

WEST VIRGINIA

Sitting alone in a bar in West Virginia watching *Monday Night Football*, I come to consider the beauty of bartenders and their metaphorical resemblance to angels. Today's incarnation is Fallon, streak of white dyed in her jet black hair, now doing shots at the bar with Rick, her sometimes boyfriend, who loves above all else playing music, always at it, only missed three days of practice in the last two years and that to go fishing with his brother. Rick is learning funk bass to accompany the bluegrass guitar he cut his teeth on back home in Nashville, which explains why he keeps requesting songs by the Red Hot Chili Peppers. *Lord, nobody in the entire state of Tennessee but plays in a band, singing about lions and buried treasure and the sweet flesh of the beloved.* Rick tells me he was born in 1984 and I tell him that in 1985 I saw the Red Hot Chili Peppers play these very songs at a club in New York City, a fact alluded to in a poem I read earlier this evening to a roomful of college students, many of whom, never having been to a poetry reading before, asked me as they exited to sign my name on their xeroxed programs, either to prove their attendance for extra credit or as if it were the autograph of a minor celebrity, a versifying Red Hot Chili Pepper descended from the library shelf. We are not far from James Wright's hometown, which can no longer afford to celebrate its famous son with the touchingly sentimental Poetry Festival named in his honor, a literary event unlike any other in this country, held in the very library in which he discovered the books that enabled his escape from that town of retired factory hands on front porch lawn chairs, a town of abandoned mills and bars not unlike this one wedged between the railroad tracks and the Ohio River. A good-looking bartender is a dangerous benefactor, bestower of mercy and temptation in like measure. Mercy which may also be oblivion. Next week I'll be sitting in a bar in central Europe drinking the local pilsner named after a golden pheasant, which I believe without ever having tasted to be delicious. Faith in the instruments and their servants, faith in good beer to come, faith that the Cowboys will lose, as they do, on a field goal in overtime. Draw a circle—whatever's inside it is the poem. Everything else is the world. Keep drawing that circle larger and larger, keep going, keep going. This poem was written on the back of a Jack Daniel's coaster at a bar in Morgantown, West Virginia, which may, after all, explain a few things.

LANGDON, NORTH DAKOTA

Just across the Red River of the North we pulled over at dusk to
watch a farm auction near Langdon, North Dakota. Pickup trucks
were parked for a quarter mile in either direction. Wind shook the
waist-high grass and weeds, lifting conic sections of dust swirling
into the white, slanting, late-summer sunlight. As we came into
the yard crowded with farmers and farmers' wives and children
the family guns were on the block: shotguns, deer rifles, down to
a bolt-action .22, "just right for a youngster." By the barn, Charlie
deciphered a family history in farm equipment: '41 tractor, '51 truck
and spreader, '72 tractor, '78 combine—good times and fallow,
all going. The auctioneer was a friend from the next county, and
the women laughed softly at his jokes, self-consciously, caught
somewhere between a wake and a square dance, while the farmers
smiled, then gazed off into the trees as if listening to the wind.
It was a wind that pulled the auctioneer's words from his mouth
and left him working his jaws broadly and soundlessly, a gray-
haired man in a cowboy hat waving his arms while the buzz of
grasshoppers from the endless fields and the noise of thrashing
leaves roared and roared. It was a dry, hard wind that blew until it
was the sound of the citizens of Langdon singing hymns in the one-
story Lutheran church at the edge of town, as their forebears had
offered up prayers of thanks a hundred years earlier at the first sight
of the borderless grasslands, moving west in the curl of the great
human wave of migration, Swedes and Norwegians off the boats
from Oslo or Narvik or Trondheim, sent out by train to the home of
relatives in Chicago—an uncle whose pickling plant already bore the
promise of great wealth—and onward, north and west, some falling
out among the prosperous lakes of Wisconsin, the meadows and
pinewoods of Minnesota, the white birch forests like home and the
green hills like heaven, through the last of the moraine and glacial
defiles, across the lithe Mississippi and into the edge of the vast
prairie, the Great Plains of North America still raw with Sioux and
locust plagues, the last massive buffalo hunts flashing in the hills of

Montana no more than a generation gone, the Arctic wind massing a thousand miles to the north and barreling down the continent, along the width and breadth of grass, the Dakotas, Nebraska, sod and wild flax in spring, limitless land, a place to plant and sow that neither Indians nor winters fierce as Stockholm's nor the virulent range wars could take away from the Vorlegs and Johannsens and Lindstroms, a tide of settlers moving out across the heartland, naming lakes for Icelandic heroes, founding towns like Fertile and Walhalla, islands in the great grass delta. It was the sweet wind of Capitalism in the inland Sargasso.

The auction began at noon, was almost over when we arrived. Gone already were the canoe, wading pool, camper, motorcycles, lawn furniture, toys, old clothes, the house, the land itself. Through the window I could see a stag's head over the mantel. Charlie's boots were thick with dust. As we left they were auctioning off an artificial Christmas tree, a last-ditch offering from Sears or Woolworth's. "A real handy article, folks, only gotta wait four months to get your money's worth—do I hear a dollar, do I hear four bits?"

It is nearing the day the smiling auctioneer spoke of, that promised Christmas, a season of hope and redemption. I have carried the draggled plastic tree across the continent and back in my heart. I have felt the silvered needles sting, heard them rustle in the glow of blinking Christmas lights like wheat fields in the first wind of autumn. It is a wind which carries the seeds of life and the dust of extinction. I have dreamt of tinsel and glass balls, of a living room in the heart of the Great Plains. It is a winnowing wind. It is a bitter wind.

DELPHOS, OHIO

is where we turned around, surrendered to fate, gave in to defeat
and abandoned our journey at a town with three stoplights, one
good mechanic, and a name of possibly oracular significance.

Which is how we came to consider calling the baby Delphos.

Which is why we never made it to Pennsylvania, never arrived to
help J.B. plant trees on the naked mountaintop he calls a farm,
never hiked down the brush-choked trail for groceries in the
gnomic hamlet of Manns Choice, never hefted those truckloads of
bundled bodies nor buried their delicate rootling toes in the ice and
mud of rocky meadows.

Blue spruce, black walnut, white pine, silver maple.

And that name! Manns Choice. Finger of individual will poked in
the face of inexorable destiny.

Which is how we came to consider calling the baby Hamlet, Spruce,
or Pennsylvania.

But we didn't make it there. Never even got to Lima or Bucyrus,
let alone Martins Ferry, let alone West Virginia, let alone the
Alleghenies tumbled across the state line like the worn-out molars
of a broken-down plow horse munching grass in a hayfield along
the slate-gray Juniata.

Because the engine balked.

Because the shakes kicked in and grew like cornstalks hard as
we tried to ignore them, as if we could push that battered blue
Volvo across the wintry heart of the Midwest through sheer
determination.

Which is foolish.

And the man in Delphos told us so.

Fuel injector, he says. Can't find even a spark plug for foreign cars in these parts. Nearest dealer would be Toledo or Columbus, or down the road in Fort Wayne.

Which is Indiana. Which is going backwards.

Which is why they drive Fords in Ohio.

Which is how we came to consider calling the baby Edsel, Henry, Pinto, or Sparks.

Which is why we spent the last short hour of evening lurching and vibrating back through those prosperous bean fields just waiting for spring to burst the green-shingled barns of Van Wert County.

Which is how we came to consider calling the baby Verna, Daisy, Persephone, or Soy.

By this time we're back on the freeway, bypassing beautiful downtown Fort Wayne in favor of the rain forest at Exit 11, such is the cognomen of this illuminated Babel, this litany, this sculptural aviary for neon birds, these towering aluminum and tungsten weeds,

bright names raised up like burning irons to brand their sign upon the heavens.

Exxon, Burger King, Budgetel, Super 8.

Which is how we came to consider calling the baby Bob Evans.

Which is how we came to consider calling the baby Big Boy, Wendy, Long John Silver, or Starvin' Marvin.

Which is how we came to salve our wounds by choosing a slightly better than average motel, and bringing in the Colonel to watch *Barnaby Jones* while Elizabeth passes out quick as you like

leaving me alone with my thoughts and reruns

in the oversized bed of an antiseptic room on an anonymous strip of indistinguishable modules among the unzoned outskirts of a small Midwestern city named for the Indian killer Mad Anthony Wayne.

Which is why I'm awake at 4 A.M. as the first trucks sheet their thunder down toward the interstate.

Which is when I feel my unborn child kick and roll within the belly of its sleeping mother, three heartbeats in two bodies, two bodies in one blanket, one perfect and inviolable will like a flower preparing to burst into bloom,

and its aurora lights the edge of the window like nothing I've ever seen.

A DOVE

If May is the month of the mockingbird, September is the season
of the dove. On the roof they have gathered to drink from warm
puddles of yesterday's rainwater, preening and cooing in the
shade, while their brothers the pigeons line the telephone wires in
radiant sunshine, waiting for their daily feed to spill forth from Mr.
Johnson's sack of seed and cracked corn. Sunday morning, 10 A.M.
High African clouds in the west, allamanda spilled in yellow spikes
and coils across the fence. In the backyard: a neighbor's cat. At the
sound of the opening window it flees, startled, then hesitates at
the top of the wall to glance back—at what?—and as my eye tracks
its gaze I catch a sudden motion in the overgrown grass, frantic
circling too big for a lizard, too desperate, and even as I notice
it and begin to speak, even as I call out *Hey, come see something
strange in the yard* I realize, in that instant, what it must be—a bird,
mauled, its weary struggle for survival—and wish I could unsay
it, wish I could avert the gaze of my conscience because already I
foresee the morning slipping away—a box, a warm towel, a bowl of
water, and the calls to the Humane Society, and the drive to Fort
Lauderdale to tender its fragile body to the wild animal hospital, a
shaded compound of blackbirds and parrots, box turtles and one-
eared rabbits—and now Sam has come over to watch with me and
I cannot will away the obvious, and he dashes out the back door
to investigate, and now the day has been taken from us, seized,
wrenched away, a day of rest I would covet even against that ring of
blood and spilled feathers, the slender broken bones in the lawn,
and now we are drawn into the circle of its small life, obligated by
our witness, impossible to deny or retract, committed long before
the dull slow course of a thought can be born into language, before
the image is set into words, as Sam's words come to me now across
the hot summer grass: *Dad, it's alive. A kind of bird. It's hurt. A dove.*

THE LEATHERBACK

I'm still slogging Sam's surfboard across the sand when the boys race off to see what the commotion up the beach is all about, and by the time I get close they've run back to report, a sea turtle, a leatherback, the biggest of them all, we've never seen one before, but there's a problem, it's injured, they've already loaded it into the back of the Fish & Game Department pickup truck as the local cops pointlessly holler to stand back, stand back, and it is truly huge, like an old sequoia log, like the barnacled hull of an overturned rowboat, one of the rangers says it is probably eighty years old, and the boys say its fins are all chopped up by a boat, but the ranger says no, a knife, and now I can see sinewy stumps where the flippers should be, gray flesh marbled with milk-white fluid, sickening, I turn away, it must have washed here from some place where turtles are still a food source, the Bahamas are less than a hundred miles east, there's a strong wind blowing Portuguese men-o'-war up on the beach, sea turtles eat jellyfish, the tentacles blind them as they age, these waves have brought us all here today, some surfers already out, others in the crowd talking about the turtle, I'm turning to head back when I see the bad look on Elizabeth's face, some of the white-haired retirees from the next building are telling her the full story, it crawled from the ocean at dawn, it didn't lay eggs, it didn't swim away, they thought it was old, maybe sick, they called the police, the fishermen from the jetty wandered over to look, one man rode it like a horse, before it's clear what's happened, or why, a fishing knife emerges to saw through the rubbery, elephant-thick skin, three flippers gone before anyone stops him, the senior citizens are shouting out, hey, no!, accosting him, what are you doing? why did you do this? and he: *for soup,* some of the old people are crying, they chase him away, get lost!, you're crazy, how would you feel if we cut your arm off like that?, some of the fishermen laughed, some shook their heads, the police arriving helpless, uninformed, it's more than I can handle, honestly, I turn away, I am trembling not with anger but with shame, the ranger truck spins its wheels and bogs down in soft sand having traveled perhaps fifty feet, it takes an hour before a tractor comes to tow them clear, the giant turtle is that heavy, what is there to say?, eighty years old, for soup, that milky extrusion—was it blood?, as I dive into the water I am thinking how generous the ocean is in its forgiveness, I am thinking at least I never looked into its eyes.

SQUID

What could ever equal their quickening, their quicksilver jet pulse
of arrival and dispersal, mercurial purl and loop in the fluid arena
of the floodlight toward which they had been lured like moths to
their undoing? We were eighteen that summer, Mike and I, working
on an old Greek-registered freighter carrying holds full of golden
corn to Mexico, corn that flowed like ancestral blood through the
continent's veins and south, down the aorta of the Mississippi, to
be loaded for transport across the Gulf. From Baton Rouge it was
hours threading the delta and one long night suspended between
stars and the galaxies of luminescent plankton stirred up in our
wake and then a week at anchor awaiting a berth in the harbor at
Veracruz. By the third day the sailors had grown so restless the
Captain agreed to lower the gangway as a platform from which
to fish for squid, which was not merely a meal but a memento of
home flashing like Ionian olive leaves. Ghost-eyed, antediluvian,
they darted upward, into the waiting, handheld nets, and then
the sailors dropped everything to dash with their catch toward
the galley like grooms carrying brides to a nuptial bed, one slit
to yank the cartilage from white-purple flesh tossed without
ceremony into a smoking skillet, trickled with lemon and oil, a
pinch of salt, and eaten barely stilled, still tasting of the sea that
had not yet registered its loss. That's the image that comes back to
me, the feast of the squid, and thereafter we passed our evenings
playing cards or ferried into port after a dinner of oily moussaka
by one of the ancient coal-burning tenders that made the rounds
like spark-belching taxis among the vessels lying at anchor, and
the gargantuan rats drinking from the scuppers, and the leering
prostitutes in the harbormaster's office, and the mango *batidos* Mike
preferred to beer, and the night we missed our ride back to the ship
and walked until the cafes closed and slept at the end of a long
concrete breakwater, and the sky at first light a scroll of atoms, and
the clouds at dawn as if drawn from a poem by Wallace Stevens,
tinct of celadon and cinnabar and azure, and the locals waking on

benches all around us, a whole neighborhood strolling out to squat and shit into the harbor, and then, piercing the clouds, aglow with sunlight for which the city still waited, the volcano—we'd never even guessed at its existence behind a mantle of perpetual mist—Pico de Orizaba, snow-topped Citlaltépetl like the sigil of a magus inked on vellum, and everything thereafter embellished by its hexwork, our lives forever stamped with that emblem of amazement, revelation, awe.

PRAIA DOS ORIXÁS

for Robert Hass

1

Farther north we came to a place of white sand and coconut palms,
a tumbledown government research station, seemingly abandoned,
no one in sight but sea turtles lolled in holding tanks along the
edge of the beach. The ocean was rough, riptides beyond a shelf of
underlying rock, water a deep equatorial green. We swam. Rested.
Hid from the sun in the shade of the palms. A few miles on we
found the fishing village by the inlet, the small restaurant with
platters of squid and giant prawns on a terrace overlooking the
harbor, manioc, sweet plantains, beans and rice in the lee of the
cork-bobbed nets and the tiny cerulean and blood-orange fishing
boats sheltered in the crook of the breakwater's elbow. A boy selling
sugarcane rode past on a donkey; white-turbaned women bent like
egrets to the salt marsh. "There is no word for this in English," said
Elizabeth,

meaning, by *this,* everything.

Later: goats and dogs on barbed-wire tethers; children laughing
beneath banana leaf umbrellas;

women hanging laundry on a red dirt hillside in a stately ballet
with the wind.

2

The next day we headed back to the city, following the rutted dirt
road along the coast until forced to a halt with the engine of our
rented Volkswagen thumping and billowing a fatal tornado of
smoke.

Fan belt, snapped in two.

It was difficult making ourselves understood in that place; they seemed to speak some backwoods dialect, or else the language failed us completely; neither Anna's schoolbook Portuguese nor J.B.'s iffy favela slang brought any clear response. People beneath strange trees ignored us in the darkness, or watched with an air of unhappy distrust, or disdain, or possibly compassion.

Although we couldn't see the beach, a sign by the road read *Praia dos Orixás.*

Eventually, one man took pity upon us, running home and returning with a fine black fan belt fresh in its package, a fan belt big enough for a tractor, impossible to jury-rig to that clockwork machine, and yet no matter how we contrived to explain ourselves, no matter what gesticulations we employed, what shadow play, what pantomime, we could not make him see that his gift would not suffice. *No good! Too big!* We held the broken belt against his, to display their comic disparity, but the man only smiled and nodded more eagerly, urged us to our task of fitting the new piece, happy to be of assistance, uncomprehending. *Won't fit! Too big! Thank you, friend!*

Hopeless.

In the end, money was our undoing, those vivid and ethereal Brazilian bills stamped with the figures of undiscovered butterflies and Amazonian hydroelectric dams. I forget whose idea it was to pay the man for his kindness, but no sooner had the cash appeared in our hands than he at last gave vent to his anger and frustration, insulted by our mistaken generosity, hurling epithets that needed no translation, and so, as the crowd approached, menacingly, from the shadows,

or perhaps merely curious, or possibly protective,

we jumped in the car, still smiling, waving our arms like visiting dignitaries, desperate to display the depths of our goodwill but unwilling to risk the cost of further miscommunication,

and drove away with a gut-wrenching racket into the chartless and invincible night.

3

What follows is untranslatable: the power of the darkness at the center of the jungle; cries of parrots mistaken for monkeys; the car giving up the ghost some miles down the road; a crowd of men with machetes and submachine guns materializing from the bush, turning out to be guards from a luxury resort less than a mile away; our arrival at Club Med; the rapidity of our eviction; our hike to the *fazenda* on the grounds of the old mango plantation where we smoked cigars and waited for a ride; the fisherman who transported us home with a truckload of lobsters bound for market.

By then another day had passed.

It was evening when we came upon the lights of the city like pearls unwound along the Atlantic, dark ferries crossing the bay, the patio at the Van Gogh restaurant where we talked over cold beer for uncounted hours. That night was the festival of São João, and the streets snaked with samba dancers and the dazzling music of *trios elétricos,* smell of roasting corn and peanuts, fresh oranges, firecrackers, sweet *jenipapo,* veins of gold on the hillsides above the city where flames ran shoeless in the fields among the shanties, warm ash sifting down upon our table, tiny pyres assembled around seashell ashtrays and empty bottles as the poor rained down their fury upon the rich. That night the smoke spelled out the characters of secret words and shadows were the marrow in the ribs of the dark. That night the stars fell down,

or perhaps it was another.

That night we yielded to the moon like migrating sea turtles given over to the tide-pull.

That night we clung together in the heat until dawn as the cries of the revelers ferried us beyond language.

That night we spoke in tears, in touches, in tongues.

KINGDOM OF THE SEA MONKEYS

When I close my eyes the movie starts, the poem rises, the plot
begins.

Falling asleep it comes to me, the novel I will never write, in
semaphore flashes against my eyelids, flames from a torpedoed ship
reflected on low clouds, flames abstract as green fingers, steam-
machinery assembled from blueprints of another era, engine-gush
of hot ash, a foliage of fears as lush as prehistoric ferns.

Up rises chaff from the threshing floor, up rises moondust, city
smoke, pulses of birdcall, voices chopped by wind into mews and
phonemes.

The mind in the true dark at 3 A.M. when the electricity goes out
with a bang—circling the ambit of consciousness, listening, probing,
defending the perimeter, as long ago, fending off wolves with
sharpened sticks when the fire died.

The perfecting of art, according to Kierkegaard, *is contingent upon the
possibility of gradually detaching itself more and more from space and aiming
toward time,*

a distinction analogous to that between perception and insight,

how the mind navigates like a bat, sometimes, soaring through its
cavern via echolocation.

Other times it rests, perfectly still, like a bowl of pond water, a pure
vessel in which the sediment, stirred up like flocks of swifts at dusk,
swirls and drifts and settles, until its next disturbance, its next
cyclonic effulgence.

Swirl, drift, settle.

It is the outside world that creates the self, that creates the sense of continuity on which the self depends—not the eyes, not the eyelash diffusing light, not the hands moving through the frame of observation, but the world.

We anchor ourselves within the familiar, like boats on an immensity of water.

Different day to day, yes—as the boardwalk of a town outside Genoa with its old carousel and honey-flavored ice cream cones differs from a plain of sagebrush in Nevada—different and yet always and immediately recognizable. Ah, there it is again, the world. And so I, too, must still be here, within the container of myself, this body, this armature. As long as I can see out I can see in.

Therefore it is only through others that we know ourselves.

Therefore the limits of our compassion form the limits of our world.

Still our lives resemble dreams, luminous tapestries woven by a mechanism like the star machine at the planetarium, realms of fantastic desire and possibility, like the kingdom of the sea monkeys promised in the back pages of comic books of my childhood, the King of the Sea Monkeys with his crown and trident, his coral-hewn castle with pennants waving. That so much could be obtained for so little! And then the licking of postage stamps, and the mailing away, and the waiting.

Or perhaps it is less like a dream than a visionary journey,

to pilot the vehicle of consciousness through the turmoil of reality as if crossing the heart of a continent, shadow of a hawk on asphalt clear as a photograph

as you rise from rich valleys into snowy mountains, black trees, meltwater, the striations of snow melting around the tree trunks like the growth rings within the wood of the trees themselves, layered accretions, historical pith.

Such a sad awakening it was, the day the sea monkeys arrived in the mail, no proud sea monarch or tiny mermaid minions, no castle, no scepter, no crown, just a little paper packet of dried brine shrimp which, tumbled into a fishbowl, resembled wriggling microscopic larvae, resembled sediment in pond water, swirling and drifting and settling.

Where is the King of the Sea Monkeys, the ruler of all memory?

Lost, and with him his kingdom, vanished like Atlantis beneath the waves, while we cling to life rafts and tea chests amid the flotsam,

old movies projected like messages in bottles within the green-glass lyceums of our skulls.

Awakening, yes, as if startled from a dream.

As when, driving in heavy rain, you cross beneath an overpass and the world leaps with mystifying clarity at the windows of your eyes.

PHILADELPHIA

Late dinner at a dark cafe blocks from Rittenhouse Square, iron pots of mussels and Belgian beer and a waiter eager to snag the check and clock out. Such are the summer pleasures of his work— winding down to a glass of red wine, catching the windowed reflection of a girl as she passes, counting the take upon the bar, thick roll of ones and fives, palming the odd ten smooth against zinc and polished walnut, the comforting dinginess of American money, color of August weeds in a yard of rusting appliances, hard cash, its halo of authority, the hands' delight in its fricatives and gutturals, its growl, its purr, gruff demotic against the jargon of paychecks on automatic deposit with social security deductions and prepaid dental, realism vs. abstraction, a gallery of modest canvasses, more landscapes than still lives, steeples of the old city with masts and spars, a vista of water meadows with fishermen hauling nets in the distance, women collecting shellfish in wicker panniers. It yields enough to sustain us, after all, the ocean of the past. We've paid. The waiter pockets his final tip and throws down his apron and walks out into the warm night of dogs splashing in public fountains and couples on benches beneath blossoming trees and soon enough we follow, arm in arm across the cobblestones, looking for a yellow cab to carry us into the future.

TABERNACLE, NEW JERSEY

is not the place I thought it was. All these years, crossing the dwarf-pine coastal midlands, the map of New Jersey gone AWOL from the road atlas, what I'd remembered as Tabernacle was actually Chatsworth, two old colonial towns, ten miles apart, peas in a pod, nothing could be more similar and nothing could be more distinct. Chatsworth, I guess, was named by the homesick for a town left behind in England, while Tabernacle implies not only a house of worship but a sanctuary and a shelter, a dwelling place and a covenant, an immaculate coal in the hearth of the New World, invested today in exurban restoration, garden centers and antique marts, new subdivisions in the old peach orchards, the historic church signed and posted for day-trippers out from Philadelphia. Tabernacle is a sign of things to come while Chatsworth is purely a thing of the past, a place so momentary its passage is forgotten even before its official contemplation—was that it?—ramshackle houses set back beneath shade trees, front porches sagged and winded, a poster for the annual BBQ & turkey shoot at the Antler Hall, a roadhouse and general store at the crossroads of the Pine Barrens, that comical backwater of forgotten towns, Batsto and Ong's Hat, Leektown and Double Trouble, so named when muskrats gnawed through the town dam two times in a single month. Muskrats. Twice.

What I like about Chatsworth is its sandy transience, its ageless and indelibly American dereliction. People came to Chatsworth, lived for a while, and moved on. They settled down, hunted deer, kilned bricks, scrounged the deposits of pig iron from the soil, harvested the cranberry bogs, chopped down the pine trees and burned them for charcoal, raised up kids for a generation or two, then headed out for greener pastures, taking Chatsworth with them and leaving Chatsworth behind. A town like Chatsworth could be anywhere, right at home among tired Tidewater tobacco fields or the chicken houses of the Eastern Shore, along the old wagon roads at some ford of the Potomac, the Susquehanna, the Delaware, the James, anywhere at all in the majestic and underappreciated Mid-Atlantic region, which is home to me, central and definitive, though for that matter you could find Chatsworth in most of Appalachia and scattered throughout the South, and into the riverine Midwest, Ohio and Illinois and Missouri and Iowa, and so into the plains, and following the Oregon Trail across the mountains and into the apple orchards of the Pacific Northwest, and even in the altogether unnatural badlands of Utah where, once, lonely to the point of desperation, I passed through just such a place on a Sunday afternoon when the volunteer firemen's picnic was in progress, a group of families eating hot dogs and buttered corn, some kids with red and yellow balloons, people waving in kindly invitation as I slowed to a crawl, and thought about stopping, and drove on.

Listen, I've driven all over this country, I've spun the odometers of a dozen bad cars, I don't know how many road atlases I've worn to sacrificial shreds, but in each and every one New Jersey opens like a flower, dead center, stapled twice through the heart. Thus it is median and first to weaken. Until one sad and inevitable day the Garden State disappears forever, lost blossom of weary abandonment. Which is why for all these years I mistook Chatsworth for Tabernacle, driving blind across the heart of the state to our cherished summer weeks at the shore, stopping for tomatoes at the Green Top Market, for frozen yogurt at the Dairy Bar in Red Lion, steered by memory from landmark to landmark along 206 or 70, 532 or 563, it hardly matters which road you take, it hardly matters the number or the sign, because even without a map I can find it, nameless or mistaken, bypassed or misplaced, past or future, beginning or end, north or south or east or west, because Chatsworth is everywhere and Chatsworth is everything: dwelling place, covenant, congregation, tabernacle.

MEMPHIS

Were we in town for the Elvis to-do? *We sure were.* Did we go to the midnight vigil last night? *We sure did.* How did we all like it? *Wonderful.* Every time she went there she got chills. *We knew what she meant.* She thinks Graceland is about the most moving place she ever was. Just looking at all those things, knowing they were his things, like the cup he drank out of, the mirror he looked into, his little fuzzy pillows, his toothbrush. It was a shame. He would of only been fifty years old this year, too. He was the King, though, he surely was . . . Well, did we like our catfish? *You bet.* More coffee? *No thanks.* Y'all have a nice time in Memphis now. *We will.*

In fact, we had a miserable time. We drove all day and night and day again to get there from L.A. Albuquerque was a net of lights, magnificently purple in the first tinting of dawn. You slide down into its web from the high plains then back into mountains. And Arkansas at night, picking up the fringe of some tropical storm system, wipers singing that blue tune, coffee from truck stops and 7-Elevens, Woody Guthrie and Black Flag and Elvis on the Walkman. We slept in the car, with Charlie's surfboard tied to the roof, in the parking lot across the street from green-and-orange-lit Graceland, after the other six thousand mourners left the gates. All those candles, and flower hearts, and women in raincoats crying, hysterical women with bright lipstick, and their husbands in toupees—from his hometown, too, Tupelo, Mississippi—and troops of women sweeping rose petals into the gutter afterwards, members of the Elvis Fan Club, Memphis Chapter, as we tried to sleep in the stifling humidity, the drone of rain and mosquitoes.

In the morning we fought our way into the very first tour group. All I remember is how small-time the place seemed, just a country house, really, the almost pathetic homeliness of it. No guitar-shaped swimming pool, no solid gold Cadillac. Just the TV he always watched while he ate. A statue he gave to his mama.

Racks of spangled, American eagle jumpsuits. We left town right afterwards. Rain all the way home through Tennessee, the tangled hills of Virginia, the storm building up to hurricane strength, past the terrible battlefield at Shiloh, and later Bull Run, places where Americans died in a roar of musket fire, all night through the relentless weather, Hurricane Elvis we call it, until even coffee won't do, or the sad songs of dust, Woody Guthrie singing about the Grand Coulee Dam, Johnny Cash with "Folsom Prison Blues," long miles of rain in the Appalachian night, dirges for the fallen, and into Washington as gray light broke from the east.

BAKER, CALIFORNIA

How many times through the suburbs of loneliness, isolated galaxies of vitriol and salt? How many times this transfigured iconography, the dry hum of terror and desolate generation? Trona, Kelso, Baker, how many journeys unto the gates of Death Valley? How many nights without refuge before one is forever marked and transformed? If the desert burns it is a property of darkness, windspur and cloven hoof, thistle like the portal of violet resolve. If the night reveals its inner self it is a property of vision, a kind of violent light, sheer and lapidary, gas stations, restaurants, assembled legions of last-chance motels, nothingness amid the nothingness of everything and nothing. *Ultraviolet* is the world I'm looking for. The *word*. It is the word I'm looking for. The moment, the place, the power and righteousness of a certain melody, not even needing to believe its dark intransigence but hear and glory in it only, the moment when noise begins to resemble music, when music comes to resemble noise. This journey, that journey, burdens and joys as hallucinatory as heat waves, the past a mirage of irredeemable distance, the place where light crosses over to water, where water reduces to light. How many times such transubstantiation? Angel of chaparral, angel of mercury vapor, how even to talk about those days now?

Years later, Elizabeth and I came upon it like a vision in the wilderness, checked into the same room at Arnie's Royal Hawaiian, the same tepid shower, the same beer and pretzels from the Stop N Go store. It was late, pitch black for hundreds of miles, and lovely in the false blue light of palm trees and neon, the rich green glow of the swimming pool. Try as I might, there was nothing I could say or do to convince her how terrible this place was, how abject a seat of desolation, why it signified despair and the madness despair brings down like unearthly snow. On TV, black-and-white helicopters circled the latest disasters: a train wreck, a toxic spill, a forest fire raging out of control in some wild scrub hills outside of—outside of

Baker, comes a voice above the buzz of copter blades, the whole town of Baker could be at risk, is all we hear, before the audio sheers to static. Once, in New York, I saw two planes collide in midair: walking along the dock at 79th Street, deep indigo Hudson River dusk, suddenly looking up to a ball of flame, a blur, objects tumbling along divergent arcs like dancing partners slipping their moorings; the first crashing in flames atop the Palisades, starting up small ruby tongues that dozens of fire engines struggled to control over the next three hours; while the second vanished beyond the Heights, a palpable concussion as it hit and exploded among oil tanks miles away in New Jersey. I saw this, and I tell you, that moment in Baker was stranger. In room 106, all is still but the air conditioner. Beyond the window: night, blue palm trees, nothing. On TV: images of flame, multitudes of flame, silent minions and consorts of flame. We move outside to the parking lot and stare into the impervious darkness. Nothing. The ice machine whispers erotic riddles, the edge of something almost cool passes over us in the breeze. Nothing. When we come to the pool we take off our clothes, part the brilliant water, immerse our bodies in its radiance until they transform to fluid emeralds.

Baker, California, is not hell, though it bears a family resemblance. That night was no infernal mime, though it carries still a tinge of the otherworldly. The forest fire burned in Baker, Oregon, a place I'd never heard of, absurdly far away, and by morning the firefighters had brought it under control. Exhausted, we slept late, and when we opened the door the dry heat sucked the night's memory from our lungs. The sun was a hammer that bent our bones like iron bars in a forge. Heat-shimmers hissed audibly as they rose in swells to fuse with the roar of traffic and vanish in the colorless vacancy of the sky. Song of the oven of days. Song of the soul in the furnace of the body. At our feet, the desert begins. The grass gives out, the parking lot peters into dust, the endless gray ruined skin of the world runs off into eternity. And there is nothing I can say or do to help you.

NORTH CAROLINA

The more you allow the figures of black, silent trees glimpsed by night from the window of a train near Fayetteville into your heart, the greater the burden you must carry with you on your journey, and the sooner you will come to question your ability to endure it, and the stronger your conviction to sing.

MANITOBA

Ten miles in we came upon the locusts, road striped and banded
with them, fields plagued and shadowed with their mass, fulsome,
darker than cloud-dapple, slick as shampoo beneath the wheels. In
the next town we stopped to scrape them from the radiator with
our pocketknives. Grasshoppers, their bodies crushed and mangled,
scaled, primordial, pharaonic, an ancient horde of implacable
charioteers, black ooze caking the headlights to blindness, mindless
yellow legs still kicking. Not much in that town: sidewalks grown
with goldenrod, grain elevator on the old railroad siding. Not much
besides wheat and gasoline, the ragged beauty of the heat-painted
prairie, wind with the texture of coiled rope, the solitude of the
plains unrolling beyond limit of comprehension. It was time to hit
the road. Charlie grabbed a root beer; I topped up the oil. We hosed
out the dead and drove on.

RICE & BEANS

"Dad?" Yes. "You are a wimp." That's very nice, thank you. Eat your grilled cheese. "I say you are a *little* wimp. I learn that at school. From a *big* kid." Of course. "Tyrannosaurus Rex, King of the Dinosaurs!" Sam is not yet three. When he roars I stick a spoonful of rice and beans into his mouth. "Dad, did Rex eat ricey-beans?" I think so. "No! He was a *meat* eater." That's right. "They *think* he was a meat eater." Who? "*Scientists.* Dad?" Yes. "Does beans have bones?" No. "Do cheese have bones?" No. "Why do they change the name of *bronto*saurus to *apato*saurus?" I honestly don't know. "*Scientists* know. They know, Dad." Yes. Probably. Drink some water, please. "Dad, water does not have bones." True. "Water does not have hands." Right. "Usually, dogs have no hands. But Scooby-Doo have hands. Why, Dad?" He's not a real dog. "Did he *die out*?" He's just a cartoon dog. "Do Scooby-Doo eat ricey-beans—*cartoon* ricey-beans?" No. Yes. Probably. I think so. Eat your sandwich. "Dad, I no call you little wimp before. *Rex* call you little wimp." That's not a nice thing to call someone, is it? "Rex is not nice. Rex *mean!*" Sam roars and I stick a crust of sandwich in his mouth. "Dad, can I have a cookie? Vanilla cookie? *Please.*" You haven't finished your grilled cheese, have you? "That's just the bones, Dad. *Toast* bones."

AMERICAN NOISE

Boxcars and electric guitars; ospreys, oceans, glaciers, coins; the
whisper of the green corn kachina; the hard sell, the fast buck,
casual traffic, nothing at all; nighthawks of the twenty-four-hour
donut shops; maples inflamed by the sugars of autumn; aspens
lilting sap yellow and viridian; concrete communion of the clover
leaves and interchanges; psalms; sorrow; gold mines, zydeco,
alfalfa, 14th Street; sheets of rain across the hills of Antietam;
weedy bundles of black-eyed Susans in the vacant lots of Baltimore;
smell of eggs and bacon at Denny's, outside Flagstaff, 4 A.M.; bindle
stiffs; broken glass; the solitary drifter; the sprinklers of suburbia;
protest rallies, rocket launches, traffic jams, swap meets; the Home
Shopping Network hawking cubic zirconium; song of the chainsaw
and the crack of the bat; wheels of progress and mastery; tugboats,
billboards, foghorns, folk songs; pinball machines and mechanical
hearts; brave words spoken in ignorance; dance music from the
Union Hall; knots of migrant workers like buoys among waves or
beads in the green weave of strawberry fields around Watsonville;
the faithful touched by tongues of flame in the Elvis cathedrals
of Vegas; wildflowers and anthracite; smokestacks and sequoias;
avenues of bowling alleys and flamingo tattoos; car alarms,
windmills, wedding bells, the blues.

CAPITALIST POEM #25

This is the dichotomy: on the one hand something from childhood.
For instance, well—Superman. That is: more powerful than a
locomotive . . . ; faster than a speeding . . . ; able to—(this is it)—
change the course of mighty rivers. Like the Grand Coulee Dam.
And the people come from all around to see it, the largest tourist
attraction in the Pacific Northwest, families from Seattle, Portland,
all the way from Bismarck, North Dakota. And FDR created the
CCC, which hired Woody Guthrie to come on up and write some
songs about the boys involved in the electrification project, a
great building and damming and tearing down of trees along the
sinuous Columbia choked with logs. And Teddy Roosevelt created
the National Parks so you could camp next to the family playing
Scrabble in their Winnebago at a reservoir in Utah. And it was
Thomas Jefferson who sent out Lewis and Clark in the first place,
along the Missouri and across the mountains, and down the same
Columbia to the sea. It's a sort of dialectic. Youth and maturity.
Man against nature. Childhood or a motorboat in Utah: that's the
dichotomy.

As far as I'm concerned just about anything from TV was a more
significant cultural phenomenon of the '60s than Vietnam.
The Flintstones, or *Mission Impossible,* or *Lost in Space.* I could tell
you things about *Lost in Space* you wouldn't believe. The carrot
creatures crying *Moisture! Moisture!* The music that signals the
invisible bog monster's approach. Uncle Angus covered with
tendrils. I don't even know which are real episodes and which ones
I made up anymore. I could tell you about the Baltimore Orioles.
Roster moves, statistics, a twi-night doubleheader in August when
the hot wind curls over the top of the bleachers and Eddie Murray
wins the first game with a two-run double in the 8th. Between
games the lines for beer and nachos are filled with laughing,
smiling people exchanging jokes, weighing the season's prospects,
savoring the victory. The second game is a pitching duel, scoreless

through nine, until Jim Palmer tires and gives up a run in the top of the 10th and leaves to a standing ovation. As the Orioles come to bat the crowd hums with energy, excited but not at all nervous, certain of victory in fact, because this is the magic summer of 1979 and fate is on the side of Baltimore. Inevitably, the Orioles get two men on, and with two out, Eddie Murray comes to the plate. Ed and Charlie and I are up screaming, Memorial Stadium chants in unison—*Edd-ie, Edd-ie, Edd-ie*—and when Eddie swings at a 1–1 pitch we know it's gone even before the ball rockets off his bat in a tremendous arc, moving slowly and even gently through the air, perfectly visible, stage-lit against the deep green of the grass, the right fielder not moving, just turning his head to watch it go, and it's like the perfect arc of youth, a constellation made up of baseball, booze, girls, and loud music, and even at 19 or 22 when the stars have shifted slightly to malt liquor, loud music, women, vandalism, and sports in general, that ball is still rising, old age and death are impossibly remote, and anyway those images of hooded figures and the grim reaper with his scythe are impossibly outdated, and now death is a giant incarnation of Fred Flintstone, impossibly huge, skewering passersby on cocktail swords like giggling olives, and he roams the outfield shagging flies, pulling the ball out of the sky in midflight, laughing loud as a hyena in the yellow-and-black-spotted skin he wears like a bathrobe, and even Eddie Murray can't hit one beyond his reach as he lopes across the grass, immense and belligerent and well-intentioned, like America, clubbing his friend Barney Rubble on the head, and even if he were to slip, just once, on loose gravel near the warning track, say, we know the laws of physics, we know the parabola must start downward somewhere, and in the split second it takes to react to the home run you see that this is life, a luminous rise and a steady, frictional wearing down, a curve disintegrating in the sure pull of gravity, Eddie Murray dropping his bat and starting the slow trot around the bases, the crowd coming to its feet, the ball finally crashing into the bullpen.

And you're rising up with a great emotional surge swelling inside you. You're standing on the aluminum bench with Ed and Charlie stamping your feet. You're waving your arms wildly in the air. You're looking up, past the glowing towers of lights, at the floodlit sky. You're yelling like there's no tomorrow.

KROME AVENUE (JANUARY 17)

Flocks of ibis on old tractors in cleared fields sliding to sawgrass,

cartloads of corn, or mangoes, or clean fill dirt,

orchards of citrus and avocado, shade houses of the enigmatic orchid growers,

dusty horses in a crude corral fashioned from cypress limbs where the canal is edged with sugarcane and banana trees by the freight tracks

hard against the *Casa de Jesús,*

convicts collecting trash along the roadside in their FLA CRIMINAL JUSTICE jumpsuits with the SHERRIF'S DEPT school bus on the shoulder, joyless troopers overseeing what appears to be a collection of high school kids caught with bags of pot in the glove compartments of their Trans Ams,

security towers around the Krome Immigration Detention Center, razor wire reefs on which the rough boats of the *loas* bound for Lavilokan have run aground,

gravel quarry gouging the template, coral rock pits and barrows,

panel truck offering shrimp and stone crab claws from the Keys,

pickups selling roasted corn or watermelons, pickups heading into the fields loaded with campesinos,

faces of the Maya picking pole beans in the Florida sunshine,

Krome Avenue: the Third World starts here.

_____

Midwinter, and we have come to pick strawberries and tomatoes, flowers and herbs, our annual nod to hunting and gathering, a voyage into the remnants of agricultural South Florida, vanishing order endangered as the legendary panther. Sure enough, Rainbow Farms has been swallowed by exurbia, and we must head farther south in search of a passable field, crossing the canals where anhingas hitch their wings to hang like swaths of drying fabric beside the dye vats on the rooftops of Marrakech, tree farms and nurseries on all sides, freeholds of the Old Floridians or _ranchitos_ run by cronies of long-deposed caudillos, ranks of potted hibiscus and party-colored bougainvillea, bromeliads, queen palms, Hawaiian dwarf ixora. When we finally find a strawberry field it's late afternoon and many have given up, but there are still a few families in the rows, hunched _abuelas_ with five-gallon buckets they will never fill today, and I wander out among them and lose myself altogether.

The strawberries are not fully ripe—it is the cusp of the season—yet the field has been picked over;

we have come too early, and too late.

Lush, parsley-green, the plants spread their low stalks to flower like primitive daisies and I seek the telltale flash of red as I bend to part the dust-inoculated leaves, spooking the lazy honeybees, but mostly there is nothing, the berries are pale, fuzzed nubs. Of the rest what's left are the morbidly overripe, fly-ridden berries melted into purple froth and those just at the bursting brink of rot—in the morning, if you bring them home,

these will wear a blue-green fur, becoming themselves small farms,
enterprising propagators of mold.

But here's one perfect, heart-shaped berry, and half a row later,
three more, in the shadows, overlooked. Where has my family gone?
Where is everybody? I find myself abandoned in the fields, illumined
by shafts of sunlight through lavender clouds, bodiless, unmoored
and entirely happy.

———

White eggplant and yellow peppers—
colored lanterns of the Emperor!

Lobular, chalk-red, weevil-scarred tomatoes—
a dozen errant moons of Neptune!

Vidalia onions seized by their hair and lifted
to free a friendly giantess from the soil!

Snapdragons!
They carry the intonation of Paris

on a rainy day in May, granitic odor of pears,
consensus of slate and watered silk.

Elizabeth snips a dozen stems
with flower shears

scented by stalks of sage,
rosemary, flowering basil, mint.

From here the city is everything to the east, endlessly ramified
tile-roofed subdivisions of houses and garden apartments, strip
malls, highway interchanges, intransigent farmers holding their
patchwork dirt together with melons and leaf lettuce—the very
next field has been harrowed and scoured and posted for sale—
already in our years here it has come this far, a tidal wave of human
habitation, a monocultural bumper crop. And to the west is the
Everglades, reduced and denuded but secure, for the historical
moment, buffered and cosseted, left hand protecting what the right
seeks to destroy. And where they meet: this fertile border zone,
contested marginland inhabited by those seeking refuge from the
law or the sprawl or the iron custody of the market, those who
would cross over in search of freedom, or shelter, or belief, those
who would buy into this world and those who would be rid of it
alike in their admiration and hope for and distrust of what they
see. And what they see is this: Krome Avenue. What they see is the
Historical Moment caged in formidable automobiles gorging on
fast food, definitive commodities of the previous century to be
supplanted by what? The next Historical Moment, and the next,
like a plague of locusts descending upon the fields, or the fields
descended upon, or these fields, now, just as they are.

———

This may be the end of it, I suspect, the last year we make this
effort. The kids are getting older and less pliable, the alligators in
the irrigation canals pushed ever farther west, carrying into the
heart of the sawgrass the reflection of a world grown monstrous and
profound. If so, I will miss the scratched hands and the cucumber
vines, ranks of hibiscus focusing their radar on the sun, the taste
of stolen strawberries eaten in the rows, chalky and unwashed,

no matter their senselessness here, in fields reclaimed from subtropical swamp, these last remaining acres empty or picked over or blossoming or yet to blossom, again fruit, again spoilage, again pollen-heavy dust.

No, the Third World does not begin at Krome Avenue, because there is only one world—.

It's late. Cars are pulling out, mobile homes kicking up gravel, a ringing in my ears as of caravans crossing the Sahara resolves to Elizabeth calling on the cell phone—*Hey, where are you?* I can see her by the farm stand, searching the plots and rows, not seeing me, still drifting, afloat, not yet ready to be summoned back. *It's time to go— where have you been?*

Where have I been, can I say for certain?

Where have I been?

But I know where I am—I'm here, in the strawberry field.

Here.

I'm right here.

THE PROSE POEM

On the map it is precise and rectilinear as a chessboard, though driving past you would hardly notice it, this boundary line or ragged margin, a shallow swale that cups a simple trickle of water, less rill than rivulet, more gully than dell, a tangled ditch grown up throughout with a fearsome assortment of wildflowers and bracken. There is no fence, though here and there a weathered post asserts a former claim, strands of fallen wire taken by the dust. To the left a cornfield carries into the distance, dips and rises to the blue sky, a rolling plain of green and healthy plants aligned in close order, row upon row upon row. To the right, a field of wheat, a field of hay, young grasses breaking the soil, filling their allotted land with the rich, slow-waving spectacle of their grain. As for the farmers, they are, for the most part, indistinguishable: here the tractor is red, there yellow; here a pair of dirty hands, there a pair of dirty hands. They are cultivators of the soil. They grow crops by pattern, by acre, by foresight, by habit. What corn is to one, wheat is to the other, and though to some eyes the similarities outweigh the differences it would be as unthinkable for the second to commence planting corn as for the first to switch over to wheat. What happens in the gully between them is no concern of theirs, they say, so long as the plow stays out, the weeds stay in the ditch where they belong, though anyone would notice the wind-sewn cornstalks poking up their shaggy ears like young lovers run off into the bushes, and the kinship of these wild grasses with those the farmer cultivates is too obvious to mention, sage and dun-colored stalks hanging their noble heads, hoarding exotic burrs and seeds, and yet it is neither corn nor wheat that truly flourishes there, nor some jackalopian hybrid of the two. What grows in that place is possessed of a beauty all its own, ramshackle and unexpected, even in winter, when the wind hangs icicles from the skeletons of briars and small tracks cross the snow in search of forgotten grain; in the spring the little trickle of water swells to welcome frogs and minnows, a muskrat, a family of turtles, nesting doves in the verdant grass; in summer it is a thoroughfare for raccoons and opossums, field mice, swallows and blackbirds, migrating egrets, a passing fox; in autumn the geese avoid its abundance, seeking out windrows of toppled stalks, fatter grain more quickly discerned, more easily digested. Of those that travel the local road few pay that fertile hollow any mind, even those with an eye for what blossoms, vetch and timothy, early forsythia, the fatted calf in the fallow field, the rabbit running for cover, the hawk's descent from the lightning-struck tree. You've passed this way yourself many times, and can tell me, if you would, do the formal fields end where the valley begins, or does everything that surrounds us emerge from its embrace?

DAHLIAS

Rain. Purple dahlias in plastic buckets, sacks of topsoil, a bent trowel. A week later the snails have eaten the dahlias and when we plant coleus in their place we remember to lace the soil with poison pellets. That the world is ultimately unknowable makes images so complexly evocative. Music, sunlight through the slats of the broken window shade, perception, the apprehensible, drawn into the mystery of the senses, fingering the shards of the mosaic, pebbles flecked with tourmaline, their weight, their smoothness in the palm while the fingertips read their facets as beveled ridgelines eroded as the wave-worn striations of a seashell. Texture of our days so hard to pin down: the action figures in the bathtub and the eggshells in the sink and the *Martha Stewart Living* on the floor and the catalogs and the mall and the Jackie Chan movie we took the boys to see and the pizza restaurant where the charming Brazilian waitress brings us, as a special favor, glasses of the frozen after-dinner drink we secretly detest. Stop. Or, slow down. Hours pass, a night, a week of sickly dawns. Light doubly filtered through the palm fronds and white lace curtains to the wooden floor scored by old termite tunnels, termite colonies rising and falling, empires chained to iron wheels and slick metal cogways, pistons, belts, engines idling in vast machine sheds as the night crew emerge from their labor into fog from the ice-bound Monongahela. Snow exists only on the tar-paper roofs and the slick skins of the automobiles, quickly melted as the steam rises from their coffee and the smokestacks imply the arrow of human intention by their strict verticality against the sky's infinite and infinitely erasable vision field. Liminal. Ice on a river, forming, a journey taken, the flow, ice melting back into the stream bearing the marks of the ice-skaters on its hide, its rind, runes of elaborate randomness chiseled in frozen dust. Life in the surface of things, artifactual energy, layer upon layer, room after room, paper through the printing press overwritten with inscrutable directions, sheets cut and bound, and handled, and sold, and shelved in the great library of time, and lost, and rediscovered, and shredded to be thrown as confetti at the ticker-tape parade of a forgotten hero. Winter birds. Weeds poking up at the edge of the asphalt. Shoes piled in a basket by the door. Umbrellas, a lunchbox, a brown paper shopping bag, the familiar loops of its handles, arc of the string like the curve of the skater's trajectory and the steam from the cooling towers blown west. Or south. Deep familiarity of the house. A green candle, photographs in silver frames, impression of a canceled stamp. And in the morning Elizabeth calls us to the garden to see what our husbandry has wrought: a massacre of snails.

THE CUSTODIAN

1.

My old friend John stops by for a few days on his way to visit his older brother, dying of cancer in Tampa. Twenty years since we drank a bottle of cheap scotch together on 105th Street, talking all night about books and their power to transform the world, talking about poetry as if it might save us from the darkness. These days, we agree, there are no simple answers to be found in that bottle, though it is not the worst place to look. For over a decade John has worked as a custodian at a university in California, mopping the corridors of quiet buildings, talking with the young professors, working for the union, carrying a ring of keys to unlock darkened laboratories and libraries. He has discovered amazing things in the book stacks in the small hours of the night, hand-printed pamphlets from Mayakovsky, the plays of Sadakichi Hartmann, untranslated poems of Roberto Bolaño. Sometimes poets famous for their political commitment come to read on campus and he alone knows that the kitchen workers in that particular building are bullied and abused by a notorious boss, but they, the workers, immigrants from Laos and El Salvador, refuse to file union grievances, refuse to confront authority in any fashion, too familiar in their previous lives with its costs. That's my niche, he says, between the poets and the dishwashers. Not to bring them together but simply to bridge the distance, the space between lives and words, the passion of the mind to connect and the intransigence of the world restraining it.

2.

For lunch we go to a Peruvian restaurant in the city and eat ceviche of mussels and onions and a platter of fried shrimp and octopus with bottles of Cristal beer.

149

He would like to live in Cuzco or Lima, find a way to visit Nicanor Parra in Chile.

He would like to live in Mexico City for a while and translate young poets back and forth across that frontier.

For a couple years I trained to be a masseur, he says, at an institute run by a Japanese master, and one day I felt against my palm a pulse of wind rising from a woman's back as surely as I feel the wind on my face right now—I was looking around the room for the draft, as if it were a practical joke, but it was what it was—pure energy rising out of the body.

Why did you give it up? I ask.

People would say, *You saved my life!*—and they would mean it. I didn't want to be that person. I don't believe in saviors.

3.

The last night of his visit we sat up late talking in the backyard, John smoking his unfiltered cigarettes, our bodies marked by the passage of time but our minds still turning familiar gears, still worrying the old bones—as if the years were the transcript of a trial we could review at command, as if the mind is a prisoner and the thread of its movement restlessly pacing the corridors of a decaying labyrinth might even now be rewound and reexamined.

Consciousness is a caged tiger, John said, raging against the bars.

But the capsules of our minds open so infrequently, I said, like the air locks on some giant spaceship. We could live together like penguins, like ants, we could be bees in a hive and still not know each other.

A tree frog sat with us, balled on the windowsill, pale and wide-eyed, like a glob of uncooked pastry dough, as the winter trade winds flung the leaves of the live oak tree down upon our heads like soft axe-blows, talking about translation and semiotics and novels written on cell phones by green-haired teenagers in Tokyo subway stations, arguing about literature and how it evolves, or degrades, or transforms—does anyone still read Zbigniew Herbert the way we did, or Delmore Schwartz, or Malcolm Lowry, does anyone care about Huidobro, Tranströmer, Pessoa?—eulogizing great bookstores and the evanescence of artifacts, the long-prophesied death of the book, quotidian relic of an archaic technology.

But books have been my whole life, he said. What will we do without them?

Loneliness is everywhere, John. Not even poetry can save us.

THE GULF

Floating in the Gulf, on a hot June day, listening to the seashells sing.

Eyes open I watch their migrations, their seismic shifts and tidal seizures, as I am seized and lifted, lulled and hushed and serenaded. Eyes closed, I drift amid their resonant sibilance, soft hiss and crackle in the tide wash, ubiquitous underwater, a buzz like static, or static electricity—but not mechanical—organic and musical, metallic as casino muzak, piles of change raked together, a handful of pennies down a child's slide. Eyes open I see them rise as one with the water, climbing the ridge with the incoming surge and then, released, called back, slide slowly down the face of their calcified escarpment, the sandy berm the small rippling waves butt up against and topple over—flop, whoosh—a fine wash of shells and shell bits and shards, a slurry of coquinas and scallops and sunrays, coral chunks, tubes and frills, the volute whorls of eroded whelks, a mass of flinty chips and nacreous wafers, singing as it descends. Like mermaids, singing. But not a song. Stranger and more varied, more richly textured, many-timbred, Gregorian hymns or Aboriginal chanting, the music of Pygmies in a forest clearing, complex, symphonic, indecipherable. But not human. Elemental. Like rain. Bands of tropical rain approaching from the jungle, sweeping the tile verandah, the sheet metal roof, against the slats of the louvered window and across the floor of storm light and coffee-flavored dust—but not liquid—mineral—mountains of shattered porcelain, broken bottles en route to the furnace—but not glass and not rain and not even a rain of glass. Ice. The day after the ice storm, when the sun peeks out, and wind comes off the lake, and what has so beautifully jeweled the trees all morning breaks loose in a sequence of tumbling cascades, chiming like tumbrels and lost castanets, falling upon snow-covered cars and encrusted fences, discarded Christmas trees piled up in the alley, smelling of wet balsam, string and plastic in their hair, and forgotten tinsel, and every needle encased in a fine translucent sheath of ice, and as I reach to touch them my fingers brush the sand and my knees bump the bottom and I am called back with a start, alien, suspended, wholly conceived within that other music, body in the water like the water in the flesh and the liquid in the crystal and the crystal in the snowflake and the mind within the body like the branch within its skin of ice.

Eyes open. Eyes closed.

Floating in the Gulf, listening to seashells, thinking of the Christmas trees in the back alleys of Chicago.

THE WRECK

Again on the highway with tears in my eyes, cadenced by rhythm of concrete and steel, music of cloud vapor, music of signs—*Blue Flame Clown Rental / Color Wheel Fencing*—again overcome, again fever-driven, transported among the pylons and skid marks of the inevitable, sirens and call boxes of a life I have laid claim to with a ticket found by chance in the pocket of a secondhand overcoat. And if it should come to that, if my fate is to be splayed on an altar of steel, heart held forth on an Aztec dagger of chrome, if this, then still I say it was beautiful, the freedom and speed with which you conveyed me, the way and the will, and I won't renounce the reek of acrid rubber or deny the need that sent me there, and I will not regret the purpose, the vehicle, the white line, the choice, and I will not mistake the message for the voice.

SILT, COLORADO

The night crossing—empty ski towns, mining towns, full moon
on the light snow and Mike asleep since Denver. Dawn came over
the mountains behind us and the west appeared slowly out of the
winter air. To describe Silt would require a tactile vocabulary to
match the roiling high country, purple and dusk fading down from
the peaks: long grazing plateaus above the river, savage dun-pale
pastels, the cliffs, gulch and guyot, each shade, each stone itself.
Five horses walked through tall grass down to the young Colorado
River to drink—the ice was breaking up, mist was rising from the
water.

Then the long pull—Martian Utah, sad Las Vegas, the ponderous,
mesquite-crazed Mojave, Baker, Barstow, Los Angeles. In Barstow I
stopped for a cup of coffee. After ten minutes at the red counter the
waitress asked us all to leave. The kitchen was on fire and our coffee
was free. Looking back through the plate glass window I saw pies in
the rack: apple, cherry, coconut cream, lemon meringue. Mike sat
up and his hair was splayed with sleep as the fire engines raced past
us into the parking lot. That was Barstow. Silt is beyond me.

DAWN

A man and a woman are driving across the Great Plains of North America.

Kansas. Saskatchewan. South Dakota.

They are hundreds of miles into their journey, cocooned by speed and metal and dusk, a chrysalis of solitude and cobalt distance. They are bodiless and encapsulated as astronauts approaching the moons of Jupiter,

their radio emits a voice-storm of signals and significant noise,

by the dashboard light they can just make out the markings on the map, a grave rubbing or ghostly palimpsest,

scrim as fine as angel's hair or the latticed veins of tangerines,

images and symbols which admit of no single probable answer but function as a kind of orchestral score for the landscape sweeping invisibly past,

a notational logic of the possible.

Hiss of tires, rush of wind, cardinal hush and ordinal thrum.

Toward dawn the radio begins another cycle.

Everything is exactly as it was. They have outdistanced the stars and the plains are just as silent, gravid, ineluctable. They have received the hieratic lunar mysteries, they possess the blueprints of a thousand civilizations.

They stop the car and get out.

In the first, ashen light shapes and templates begin to appear.

A horse, a flock of doves, windrows of trees between the freshly plowed fields, distant cathedrals of grain elevators rising from the mist.

They have everything they need to create the world.

They have only to join hands. They have only to choose.

Part Four

An Odyssey
of Appetite

America's hunger takes nothing for granted.
Ants hollowing fallen fruit,
recasting the temple of the pomegranate,

mice in their congress of grain, squirrels in the heart
of a deciduous continental democracy,
mountains scored by rivulets,

granite beds, plains of salt or river clay,
subduction and production and consumption
driven by the master narrative of orogeny,

magma become lava in the instant of eruption
as a chocolate egg ruptures its shell of golden foil
in a hand that might belong to young Tom Jefferson

pursuing the butterfly of his happiness, or
Benjamin Franklin flying a kite,
or the daydreaming machinist Henry Ford

inventing the mass-market,
or you, or me, or everyone, or no one.
America's epic is the odyssey of appetite.

* * *

THE GENIUS OF INDUSTRY

Lay me on an anvil, O God.
Beat me and hammer me into a crowbar.

—CARL SANDBURG

Lost in the Wilderness,

crouched in the underbrush as the flames approached,
the rattle of muskets mingling with the cries of the wounded
caught in the creeping wildfires and burned to death,

the blindness of days
pushing further into that miasma of killing,

the men were left with little to ponder
but the character of their new Commanding General,
Ulysses S. Grant.

Surely, so the talk went
in the camp of the 5th Michigan
and the 9th New Hampshire, the 21st Ohio
and Indiana's famous Iron Brigade,
surely he would retreat.
Faced with this indecisive firefight,
thickets of scrub oak in hidden gulches,
heavy losses on both sides,
the danger of a sudden reversal
as at Chancellorsville,

surely Grant would retreat
like all the others—
McClellan and Burnside, Hooker and Pope—
move back to Washington and resupply,

prepare to fight it out again next month, or next season,
or next spring. It was only common sense.

And in the days and weeks that followed—

cold marches through the woods of Virginia,
the Bloody Angle of Spotsylvania,
the two armies locked together day and night,
grinding the life from each other
like implacable lovers—

as the men discovered that Grant would not retreat,
that Grant meant relentless battle,

it could be said that America
discovered its particular genius:
getting down to business.

As personified in Sam Grant,
a smallish, red-bearded man
seated beneath an oak tree in a dirty uniform
whittling a stick into smaller
and smaller pieces, making nothing,
it was a genius for death.
In that final struggle of the war,
a continual, yearlong skirmish from the Wilderness
to its conclusion, a sort of square dance where
the partners rushed out and fired
round after round
from twenty paces beneath a bright sun,
new men stepping up
to take the place of the fallen
while the caller whistled out directions,

do-si-do and promenade,
it was Grant who called the tune, relentlessly
and without mercy. It took the North
four years for Lincoln to find Grant,
hidden away in the heartland
getting drunk and winning battles,
and bring him east to end it.

I need this man, old bloody-handed Abe said.
He knows how to fight. He knew
that victory meant *getting down to*
the job at hand; meant relentless pressure;
meant "the maximization of the numerical advantage
and the superior productive capacity of the North."
Most of all, he knew that victory meant death,
a new, fully modern kind of death,
an industrialized democracy of killing
in the muddy siegeworks and trenches around Petersburg,
at the fords along the Pamunkey and Rappahannock,
in the slaughter at Cold Harbor
and the crossroads at Five Forks,
the last footrace with Lee's starving men
ending finally beneath the dogwoods of Appomattox
in the victory not so much of one general,
or even one army, as of a particular vision of America,
an ideology just coming into its own.

Across the distance of a century
we can see that this is what matters,
not so much the man himself
as what he signifies—though Grant
is so perfectly American,
his pragmatic strength and paradoxical weaknesses,

the love of booze and horses and cheap cigars.
Ulysses Grant was to warfare
what Henry Ford was to the automobile.
And as the military purists
even today resent Grant's lack of subtlety,
the absence of Napoleonic finesse,
we imagine the dismay
of the fine craftsmen of the Old World
laboring over their hand-tooled
products, self-righteous and scornful
of the Model T's rolling off the assembly line
and Ford thinking *fuck them*
I want to rule the world.
As after the war Grant's lieutenants,
Sherman and Sheridan, scoured the West
turning bad Indians into good ones, taming
the wilderness, making the world safe for democracy;
thus was Montana made safe for the Great Northern Railroad,
immigrants conned into settling by such extravagant claims
that the Dakotas came to be known as "Jay Cooke's Banana Belt";
thus the plains were settled and cities arose in the desert;
thus were cartels born; thus were bubbles burst;
thus General Motors and the rubber industry
got together with John D. Rockefeller
to purchase the Los Angeles interurban transit system,
one of the most modern and extensive in the country,
and dismantled it, as a public service, so that
the automobile—"the future of America"—
should have less disruptive competition,
in the process making millions for themselves at the expense
of the general public, which after all is the definition
of a great Capitalist. And O, the beautiful freeways,
the Santa Monica and the Long Beach and the San Diego!

Phoenix and Los Angeles as much a part of it
as Detroit or Pittsburgh with their
smelters and rolling mills and slag heaps,
strip mining in West Virginia
and strings of motels like diamonds in the desert
outside Gallup, New Mexico,
everything a product of the cultural assembly line.
Because it wasn't so much the machines themselves—
though the power of those cogs and wheels
to dehumanize the average Joe
should not be underestimated—
as it was a new idiom,
a new pace to American life, an endless refinement
down to some replicable pattern,
an industrialized essence,
as William Carlos Williams
hammered out language, manufacturing a poetry
pure as circuit boards. A rhythm,
waves lapping the shore of Lake Michigan
as you head south along the Drive, south
into the industrial belt,
Hammond, Gary, East Chicago,
the gas jets of the refineries, smokestacks gushing steam,
a million naked bulbs in the white glow
of phosphorus, the rumble of machinery,
sky bruised orange by the roar of production.
Or sailing up the Mississippi after dusk
between banks alive with petroleum plants,
the cabled towers of relay stations
and chemical storage facilities,
bright as day all night and
all the way up to Baton Rouge
where the giant snake-headed hoses

load corn into the deep holds of the freighter,
a mountain of chipped yellow grain,
and the fine, powdery residue
turning the cranes
and all the sailors white, dust—
corn dust—that gums your eyes shut,
an overpowering taste
that will linger all the way to Veracruz.

That afternoon, after loading, the ship
puts about and runs south, pale as talcum,
nestling deep into the water with its new weight.

By day the riverbanks are Amazonian.
The warehouses and lading bays
without their blinding electrical eyes

seem inconsequential, lost against the swampy horizon,
Louisiana sweeping past hour by hour
as you crouch hammering rust from the hull,

hearing the waters part before you,
the intonations of the mallets
on the thick steel plates, a dull ringing

of calloused hands hammering steadily
beneath the white sun while each stroke
raises a cloud of rust chips into your face

and the dragonflies settle by the hundreds
to bask on the hot metal of the deck
and then rise again at each reverberation,

rising and falling to the beat of the hammers,
the whole insect mass like an emerald
and turquoise lung, rising and falling,

the pulse of a primordial engine.

ALMOND BLOSSOMS,
ROCK AND ROLL, THE PAST SEEN
AS BURNING FIELDS

Across the highlands farmers are burning their fields
in the darkness. The fleet, infernal silhouettes of these men
and the owl-swift birds scared up from the chaff
flicker briefly against the silken curtain of flame as we pass,
an image from Goya cast once before our eyes
to be lost as the road swerves up to alabaster
groves of olives and white-knuckled *almendros*.
Hungry, exhausted, driving all night, there are four of us
hunched in the shell of the beaten, graffiti-winged Bug
that we scalped for sixty dollars in Berlin,
no shocks, bald tires, a broken starter so that
we have to pop the clutch every time, dashing like fools
through the streets of Amsterdam and Barcelona—
Hank with no accent, Dave with no license
except for his beard, Ed with the box turned all the way up,
playing over and over the only two tapes we have left
since the night of the lurid Basque luau
and street riot in San Sebastián. For whatever reason
we are insanely happy. Wild and lost, speed-mad,
high on the stale bread and cold ravioli we've eaten for days,
giddy with smoke and the echoes of flame leading south,
El Greco fingers of chalk blue and turtledove moonlight
at rest on the soft wool mantillas of distant sierras,
rock and roll working its harmonic convergence,
odor of diesel and wild cherry, almond blossoms
settling like ash to the asphalt— No. Wait.
It wasn't four. There were three of us left
after Hank stayed behind with that girl in Madrid.
And it was ash. Just there, where the highway
carried the flame's liquid insignia, an ash-blizzard

swirled and impelled itself irretrievably
into the melted tar. It was like a county road in Colorado
I once drove, coming to a place where milkweed
or dandelion spores confounded the air
and fell into the fresh-laid blacktop, embedded there,
fossilized, become the antediluvian kingdom
another era must decode. For us, all of Spain was like
anywhere else, driving the Great Plains or Inland Empire,
Los Banos, Buttonwillow, Bakersfield,
familiar rhythm and cadence of the road,
another car, another continent, another rope of lights
slung the length of the San Joaquin Valley.
I don't know if the rush we felt was culturally specific,
though it was the literal noise of our culture we rode
like Vandals or Moors toward a distant sea,
but that feeling was all we ever desired, that freedom
to hurtle madly against the sweet, forgiving flesh of the world,
urged on by stars and wind and music,
kindred spirits of the night. How the past
overwhelms us, violent as floodwaters, vivid as war.
Now Ed wears a suit and tie, Dave deals used cars
in L.A., "pushing iron," as the salesmen say.
My wife and I walk home from the grocery store
through streets of squirrels and school buses
bathed in late October sunlight, musky odor of paper bags
and fresh cheese bread from the Baltic bakery,
when the smell of someone incinerating fallen leaves
brings back a landscape of orchards and windmills,
the inscrutable plains of Castile and Estremadura.
I don't even know what they were burning out there
but it must have been the end
of the season. The symphony of years glissades
like tractors tracing figure eights across a muddy slope,

sweep and lull of machetes in the sugar fields,
Fiji or Jamaica, places Elizabeth and I have traveled since,
smelled the candied stink of smoldering cane.
But what concerns me most is not so much the smoke,
the resin and ash of human loss,
but rather how glibly and with what myopia
we bore the mantle of individual liberty across the continents,
as if our empowerment entailed no sacrifice in kind,
no weight of responsibility. I guess it was a sign
of the times. That jingoistic, reelection year
a spirit of such complacent self-congratulation reigned
that even Paris seemed a refuge from the hubris.
At the Olympic ceremonies in Los Angeles
they chose to reenact the national epic, westward
expansion, only due to certain staging restrictions
the covered wagons full of unflappable coeds
rolled from west to east, a trivial, barely noticed flaw.
It is America's peculiar gift and burden, this liberation
from the shackles of history. And we were such avatars.
We took what was given and thought, in all innocence,
that the casual largesse we displayed in return
was enough. When we parked for good in Algeciras
we left the doors unlocked, key in the ignition.
You see, the brakes were gone and it wasn't our country.
Immense in the heat-shadowed distance loomed
the glittering, mysterious mountains of Africa,
and though we stood in the very shadow of the Rock of Gibraltar
we never even noticed it. That's how I picture us still,
me and Ed and Dave on the ferry to Tangier,
laughing in our sunglasses, forgetting to look back.

COMMODITY FETISHISM
IN THE WHITE CITY

Our architecture reflects us, as truly as a mirror.
—LOUIS SULLIVAN

Looking west from the kitchen the weather is transformed. Storm
    light unrolls like a magic carpet, softens the lowering clouds,
the snow, less ominous, windless, dropping straight down on the
    alley, garages and rooftops geometrically outlined,
smokestacks, water towers, cottonwoods and maples, uniform back
    porches hammered from two-by-fours and unfinished lumber,
the backyard a pillowed expanse extruding elbows and rockers of
    the overturned aluminum patio chairs,
a charnel yard emerging from monsoon mud or a battlefield
    reclaimed by creeping sand dunes.

Thirteen days without sun, terminal overcast stalled above the city
    like a shield to protect us from what we most desire.

Iron gray.
Relentless.
Chicago.

My father tells me there is a depressive syndrome called seasonal
    affective disorder—SAD—which means the midwinter blues,
which means we are, like flowers, heliotropic, subject to solstice,
    attuned to equinox and perihelion,

which means we're even weirder
than we think we are.

Cushion of snow on the window ledge, whistling teakettle, steam
    like the ghost of Hot Chocolate Past:

feels like a day off from school, license to curl up in blankets and
    watch *The Price Is Right* until Mom comes home.

•

Hey, I think I'll enjoy this
tasty repast
in front of the tube!

Let's see now: leftover
Chinese
or liverwurst and Swiss?

•

Look, that dog food's packed
with real beef gravy!

Will the celebrity spokesperson eat it?

I'm still waiting for the advertising boys to break this taboo, leap
    this low hurdle, cross the frontier of bestiality
and compel Robert Urich or Lorne Greene or whichever down-on-
    his-luck former primetime star
to plunge a silver fork into those luscious nuggets and savor the
    rich, hearty flavor of all-beef goodness

just like Fido!

After all, if I won't eat it, why should he?
If it's good enough for my dog, it's good enough for me.

Such a small, such a beautifully small,
such an infinitesimally
gorgeous

abyss.

•

Of course, meat was Chicago's first great industry,

a virtual monopoly controlled by the South Side packinghouses,
    Gustavus Swift and Philip Armour and the rest of their
    cutthroat cartel,
their visionary manipulation of consumer psychology, the pickling
    vats and offal heaps laid bare by Upton Sinclair,
vast fleets of refrigerator cars at the Union Stock Yards manned by
    rock-bottom immigrant labor,

the strong-shouldered muscle the city was built upon,
the capital accumulation by which it was built,

a real killing,
any way you slice it.

If New York is an apple,
Chicago is pure sausage.

Chicago is liverwurst.
Chicago is lumber, sowbellies, soybeans, freight trains.
Chicago is the nexus where pigs and cows become puts and calls,
    where corn and copper become shorts and corners,

where wheat transforms into paper promises
premised on possible productivity,
which is to say, *the future,*

all by means of one simple equation.

Cattle drive, feedlot, slaughterhouse: Board of Trade.
Clearcut, logjam, lumberyard: Board of Trade.
Amber waves, gristmill, Wonder Bread: Board of Trade.

It's a form of modern alchemy,
a public sacrament,
an open secret!

It's a quick trip on the El to the ornate observation balconies above
    the primal trading pits in the Loop,
where you can witness the literal transmogrification of the fruits of
    earthly labor into abstract quanta
by gangs of men furiously signifying with frantic gestures the
    private glyphs of their transnumerative calculus,

a scene which never fails to remind me
of apes learning sign language
on the Discovery Channel,

their hierarchy and ritual deference,
slow mastery of sign and indicator,
the pathos of their struggle to articulate desire—

GIVE APPLE KOMBI
PLAY HIDE-AND-SEEK KOMBI
HUG KOMBI PLEASE

Chicago has an apple for Kombi,
if the price is right!

Chicago is ready to talk turkey.

Chicago is a Great Ape House gone bananas,
a Hanseatic citadel in hog heaven,
a mercantile carnation pinned to the lake's lapel,
a magic hat from which the rabbit of capital is pulled,
a portal into the realm of money itself,

and as in all border towns the locals grow rich off the unwary
    travelers they smilingly fleece and service,
and woe unto he who suffers the perils of fortune unincorporated
    into the greater risk pool of the system.

•

In December 1836, an enterprising local miller bought
up more than a thousand hogs from Sugar Creek farms
and drove them down the road to American Bottom.
Twenty miles south of the Creek a sudden drastic drop in
temperature caught him and his men, threatening them
with killing cold. As they raced in panic for the shelter of
a nearby cabin, their hogs began desperately to pile up on
each other for warmth. Those on the inside smothered,
those on the outside froze, creating a monumental pyramid
of ham, frozen on the hoof. The marketing experiment was
a dead loss and the miller financially destroyed.

—John Mack Faragher, *Sugar Creek*

•

So Chicago grew
and grew fat
off the fat of the heartland.

So it is still, more or less unchanged in its bluntly commercial
    convictions.

Rich men wear fur coats in the streets because the weather is cold
    and they are rich.
Factory workers drive Oldsmobiles because Oldsmobiles are better
    than Buicks and they don't make Packards anymore.
Unemployed factory workers move out of the city because the
    only place hiring is Wal-Mart and it's cheaper out there in the
    hinterlands of exurbia.

Chicago is your basic meat and potatoes.
Chicago is white bread.
Chicago is a monumental pyramid of ham.

•

> When man Vanuatu brought the pig with him from New
> Guinea thousands of years ago, he probably brought also
> the concept of it as the most valuable currency. With pigs
> he could ascend in status, with pigs he could acquire wives,
> with pigs he could pay for the services of sorcerers and
> artisans. The pig may not have been the most portable
> currency ever devised, but in Western Melanesia it still
> remains the most highly prized.
>
>   —Norman and Ngaire Douglas, *Vanuatu: A Guide*

•

This train of thought
is spoiling
my lunch. That's the problem

with liverwurst:
twenty minutes later you're
hungry again.

•

Speaking of ham,
Bob Hope has always been big in Chicago.
Seven shows a day at the Stratford Theater, still glamorous

in 1946. Seven shows!
The man is nothing if not a fanatic,
an indomitable trooper in the old joke factory, a faded rose

of a star-spangled performaholic,
although, like so much that we consider American,
he's an imported model, not a true domestic.

Son of a hard-drinking immigrant stonemason,
Bob passed through Ellis Island early,
en route from Bristol to his new home in Cleveland,

where he evinced a precocious talent for comedy,
a ready facility for cutting a rug,
changed his name from the original Leslie

and thus became Bob Hope the Buckeye street pug,
Bob Hope the shill at the Alhambra pool hall,
Bob Hope the wisecracking street-corner thug.

Quit school at sixteen to work in his uncle's butcher stall,
hard-knuckled, hungry, lean and pale
from the long days of ox-blood and entrails,

sour odor of meat beneath his fingernails
during tap-dance lessons at Sojack's Dance Academy
on Lake Erie evenings gray as a lunch pail,

a tenth-grade dropout with the gift of gab, an affinity
for hard work, and a dream
to escape blue-collar Ohio, a trinity

familiar to every immigrant's son, the dream
of New World wealth and glory,
the American Dream.

And the rest, as they say, is history.
Which happens to be
our story.

•

Have you noticed there's nothing on TV anymore?

Liposuction. Public prayer. Cajun food. Korean cartoons. Jane
    Goodall's chimps. The Congress.

History repeats itself.
So, too, the History Channel.

Again Grant's army encamped before Vicksburg.
Again the Gold Rush, again the Gilded Age.

Again the Wobblies, again Black Friday, again the New Deal, again
     Enola Gay.

On CNBC today, word that "gourmet pet food" is America's newest
     multibillion-dollar industry.
On CNN, an increase in global malnutrition; 40,000 children die of
     hunger and its attendant diseases every day.

Which is not to say there is any particular correlation between these
     contemporaneous pronouncements,
not to say the good citizens of Chicago would rather their dogs
     eat Veal and Kidney Morsels than the children of Pakistan eat
     rice,
not to say we can even encompass the human implications of these
     binary blips aswim in the inundation of the great data flow,
the Sea of Information from which they have arisen like walruses
     heaved up on some high blue shelf of the Malthusian iceberg.

•

I thought squirrels were supposed to hibernate.
Isn't that what they say on the Discovery Channel?
Isn't that what "the industrious hoarding of acorns" is all about?

So what's with this rigamarole in the branches?

Here's one clambering up through six inches of snow, struggling to
     drag a frozen newspaper back to its nest,
a bedraggled sheath of ads for cars or maybe tires, steel-belted
     radials from Sears or Montgomery Ward.

Alas, poor Sears, the state's largest employer, the world's tallest
    building and the city's most obvious landmark,
an unrentable white elephant boxing the Loop in sovereign shadow.
    Once upon a time they ruled the world!

Once upon a time Chicago was the general store for half the nation,
    not just day-trippers in from Wisconsin and Indiana but all
    those within reach of the mighty catalogs,
all those bicycles and reapers and Mason jars shipped out to
    pickle the beets and preserve the plums of Oklahoma, Kansas,
    Minnesota, and the Dakotas.

•

By the dawn of the new century, the Montgomery Ward
catalog contained 1,200 pages and 17,000 illustrations,
offering no fewer than 70,000 separate items for sale. . . .
The firms' yearly postal money order business was greater
than that of entire cities like Cincinnati, New Orleans,
or San Francisco. . . . By 1900, Montgomery Ward and
Sears, Roebuck were the two greatest merchandising
organizations in the world.

—William Cronon, *Nature's Metropolis*

•

When I was a kid I'd walk up to Sears to buy just about anything—

ballpoint pens or school notebooks,
a new sled, leaf bags,
a lawn mower or Doobie Brothers album.

Today, I'd as soon shoot myself as shop at Sears!

Today one must navigate daunting loops of expressway misnomers
    out to some suburban circumlocution
in order to ransack the latest jumbo, discount, wholesale Wal-or
    K-or What-the-Hey-Mart,
which is not so much a store as a merchandising organization
    disguised as an aircraft hangar lumped full of bulk
    commodities.

•

Chicago is a merchandising organization
disguised as an aircraft hangar
lumped full of bulk commodities.

•

Yes, that's true.
It is.
We are.

Materialism is our genius; must we bow down our heads in shame
    therefore?
Why apologize for seeking fulfillment in the satiation of our
    hungers?
What engine drives human history if not the elevation of physical
    comfort?
What other principle conforms to the contours of individual
    desires?
Is it not our Jeffersonian right and obligation to pursue the fleeting
    figure of happiness?

•

HAPPINESS

I asked the professors who teach the meaning of life to tell me
    what is happiness.
And I went to famous executives who boss the work of
    thousands of men.
They all shook their heads and gave me a smile as though I
    was trying to fool with them.
And then one Sunday afternoon I wandered out along the
    Desplaines river
And I saw a crowd of Hungarians under the trees with their
    women and children and a keg of beer and an accordion.

                                                —Carl Sandburg

•

Yes, Carl, how beautiful
a poem,
how telling, how fine.

But can we subsist on a diet of accordion music and raw profusion?
Is the solace of the material enough to sustain us?
At what cost has it been purchased?
Don't we crave a more elusive amplitude, a hunger no less intense
    for being nameless?
Is it possible to fix a common focus with such singularity of vision?

When I look out my window, when I look not to look but to see,
    even the most elemental forms and objects are shaded with
    hermeneutical nuance,

the unsaid, the understood, subtexts half buried by this blizzard of
    the incomprehensible,
a world of circumstance and utter contingency invested with a deep
    and apparent historical sheen.

In these arcane graffiti sprayed across the Baptist church are
    encoded the territorial markings of the local Chicano street
    gangs,
children of Oaxaca and Michoacán displaced to the frozen verge of
    Lake Michigan,
their scrawled logos imbued with intricacies of signification akin to
    Mayan sun stones or the birdman petroglyphs of Easter Island.

In these wooden houses and brick three-flats is depicted the
    evolution and degradation of the American city,
our hegemonic apogee and concomitant deliquescence, the wildfire
    of industrialization that fueled Chicago's growth,
the development of the consumer economy and the invention of the
    balloon-frame building method,
a tradition of relentless reduction to cheaper and faster means
    through the turbo-engine of mass production.

In the Housing Authority high-rise perched anomalously on
    the corner of Clark Steet is written the victory of New Deal
    liberalism and the failure of its utopian social engineering,
not to mention the aesthetic capitulation to Bauhaus hideosity its
    yellow-brick conformity embodies,
and insofar as half of its inhabitants are retired black city workers,
    and the other half ancient Japanese widows,
it reifies simultaneously the memory of the Nisei internment
    camps and the postwar movement of African Americans to the
    manufacturing centers of the North,

which in turn encompasses a brief history of organized labor,
and how the blues came up the river from Mississippi,
and the relativity of our constitutional liberties,
and the dark imponderable of slavery,

and a deeper strata of humanistic yearning in the age-old migration
    of populations in search of material betterment.

Material betterment!

I guess you could say
the writing
is on the wall, *hermano*.

You could say the writing is the wall,

our homes are our castles,
our bodies our temples,

so what metaphor must the city we live in describe?

What girders underlie the construction of the dream?
What marvels of engineering, what existential architecture?
What wrecking ball or hidden rot even now betokens its
    deconstruction?

If what we build speaks for us, what does Chicago say?

What's written in Louis Sullivan's damascened grillwork, the Sears
    behemoth, the public housing battlements, the suburbs' ever-
    increasing dominion?
What texts are affixed to the shingle roofs of the endless blocks of
    Back of the Yards bungalows?

What utilitarian tunes would the warped beams of this tired house
    hum?

What about what we haven't built,
what's been lost,
what we've built and then torn down,

the mile-high skyscraper of Frank Lloyd Wright, the bulldozed
    stockyards and Comiskey Park,
red wagons of waffle vendors at the Water Street Market and Delta
    bluesmen stomping around Maxwell Street trash fires
and the palisade of old Fort Dearborn where the Pottawatomie
    came to trade for blankets, hatchets, whiskey, and beads?

What about the White City,

the World's Columbian Exposition master-planned by Daniel
    Burnham to serve as Chicago's debutante cotillion,
a prolix effulgence of fin de siècle flotsam announcing the end of
    the nineteenth century seen as the Age of Progress through
    Industry?

If the 7-Eleven is a minnow, and Wal-Mart a bluefin tuna, the White
    City was Moby Dick.
If the 7-Eleven is a slot machine, and Wal-Mart a bingo parlor, the
    White City was Las Vegas.
If the 7-Eleven is a glittering chapel—like the beautiful Santuario at
    Chimayo—and Wal-Mart a sturdy cinder-block church of solid
    suburban parishioners,

then the White City was a metropolis of neoclassical cathedrals
    raised up to the Gods of Materialism themselves—

Manufactures, Machinery,
Electricity, Transportation, Agriculture,
Forestry, Fisheries, Mines.

Such were the pavilions wherein was gathered every conceivable
      artifact and innovation of national origin or adoptive ancestry,

every all-American doodad, gizmo, gimcrack, and curlicue,
and those of the various individual states,
and those of whichever nation or homeland cared to participate,

all and sundry jam-packed into some dozen
bulging Palladian pleasure domes,
an urban dreamscape of wings, naves, galleries, and transepts,
lagoons, ponds, basins, bridges,
wedding-cake fountains and Creamsicle statuary,

plus scores of lesser Beaux Arts repositories,
plus the carnival clutter and anthropological detritus of the
      Midway.

The murals in the Woman's Building were painted by Mary
      Cassatt.
Louis Sullivan designed the Transportation Pavilion, and later
      denounced it as an exercise in sentimental retrospection.
Eugene V. Debs saw the whole assemblage as tribute to the laborers
      that built it, among them Elias Disney, Walt's father, driving
      nails into the prototypical Magic Kingdom.
Henry Adams came back twice to plumb its mysteries; William
      Dean Howells found nirvana reflected within its Golden Door.
Frederick Douglass addressed the "Race Problem in America" on
      "Colored People's Day" when the vendors sold watermelon in
      naked mockery.

Thorstein Veblen invented socioeconomics to explain the daily
spectacle out the window of his office in the newly christened
University.
Frederick Jackson Turner announced the closing of the American
frontier in his famous derivation from 1890 census data,

the first to use punch cards for rapid tabulation,
the binary egg from which the computer was hatched,

thereby yoking the past with the future,
that century with this,
the Information Age with the vanishing Era of the Heroic
Individual,

whose incorporation into the body politic was symbolically
recapitulated in this act of appropriation, quantification, and
mythopoeic enshrinement.

Which is why cowboys blame bureaucrats and not barbed wire for
their troubles.
Which is why IBM was once the Computing-Tabulating-Recording
Company.
Which is why thirty million people visited the White City in the
half year it was open.
Which is why we speak of it as a watershed.
Which is an uncomfortable metaphor alongside the Great Lakes.

•

Since Noah's ark, no such Babel of loose and ill-joined, such
vague and ill-defined and unrelated thoughts and half-
thoughts and experimental outcries as the Exposition, had
ever ruffled the surface of the lakes.

Chicago asked in 1893 for the first time the question whether the American people knew where they were driving.

Chicago was the first expression of American thought as a unity; one must start there.

—Henry Adams, *The Education of Henry Adams*

•

Anyway, six months later they
demolished it,
or let it go to arson,

every pergola, proscenium, colonnade, and cornice,

so much unfinished confectionary,
so much frosting on a cake of illusion.

Beneath the facade the White City was built not of brick or granite
    but of sculpted plaster over lath and beams,
a temporary contrivance unfit to weather the winter, meant to look
    beautiful but not to last,
as if they'd constructed Disney World from Lego blocks and Lincoln
    logs and tore it all down at the first sign of rain,

as if it were merely a form of mass hallucination,
a collective vision of a heaven so imminent
its electric glow lit the contours of the century's horizon
with the glitter of a thousand elysian fields,

as it still does, in reverse, for us, looking backward,

a quixotic flame like a firefly encased in viscous amber,
a token of everything we have become in a dialect we no longer speak,
a beacon as perfect and irretrievable as a dream.

•

Newly arrived and totally ignorant of the Levantine
languages, Marco Polo could express himself only with
gestures, leaps, cries of wonder and of horror, animal
barkings or hootings, or with objects he took from his
knapsacks—ostrich plumes, pea-shooters, quartzes—
which he arranged in front of him like chessmen.
Returning from the missions on which Kublai sent him,
the ingenious foreigner improvised pantomimes that
the sovereign had to interpret: one city was depicted by
the leap of a fish escaping the cormorant's beak to fall
into a net; another city by a naked man running through
fire unscorched; a third by a skull, its teeth green with
mold, clenching a round, white pearl. The Great Khan
deciphered the signs, but the connection between them
and the places visited remained uncertain; he never
knew whether Marco wished to enact an adventure that
had befallen him on his journey, an exploit of the city's
founder, the prophecy of an astrologer, a rebus or a
charade to indicate a name. But, obscure or obvious as
it might be, everything Marco displayed had the power
of emblems, which, once seen, cannot be forgotten or
confused. In the Khan's mind the empire was reflected
in a desert of labile and interchangeable data, like grains
of sand, from which there appeared, for each city and
province, the figures evoked by the Venetian's logogriphs.

—Italo Calvino, *Invisible Cities*

•

City of concrete, city of illusion, how to decipher such dialectical
    ambiguity?
How can I reconcile my affection with my anger, my need to criticize
    with my desire to praise?
If there's only one Chicago, which is it: Thorstein Veblen's or Milton
    Friedman's, Gene Debs's or Mayor Daley's, Studs Lonigan's or
    Bigger Thomas's,
the White City, the Gray City, the Black city abandoned to sift
    through the ashes?

If no man is an island, why was Daniel Burnham buried on one?
If even this utopian visionary elects for himself eternal isolation
    what hope can there be for any commonweal?
What does it mean that Louis Sullivan ended in impoverished
    oblivion, tormented by the shadows of the skyscrapers he
    designed?
Can it be a mere coincidence that the balloon-frame building
    method was invented by a man named Snow—

or else Augustine Deodat Taylor,
depending on which source you credit?

Have I mentioned that the Museum of Science and Industry is in
    fact the last vestige of the Columbian Exposition,
the former Palace of Fine Arts at the great fair, the only one of the
    White City's temples built of actual stone?
Or that Lincoln logs were invented by John Lloyd Wright, first son
    of famous Frank?
What sort of diminutive Oedipal revenge is this: Laius stabbed to
    death by a toothpick, modernism brought down by Lilliputian
    arrows?

How can I account for my love of this place?
Is it simply nostalgia, that I was born here, that my son, so soon,
    presumably will be?
Could it really be as simple as fathers and sons, that ancient,
    atavistic, blood-weary principle?

What voice is this that issues from the deep well of the past?
Who calls to me from that vast assemblage?
All this, all this—

and what?

BENEDICTION FOR
THE SAVIOR OF ORLANDO

Signs and wonders: *Jesus Is Lord Over Greater Orlando*
snake-tagged in cadmium on a vine-grown cyclone
fence along I-4 southbound north of downtown
is a credo that subverts the conventional wisdom
that Walt Disney is the messiah and his minions the christened
stewards of this place, that the Kingdom to Come shall be Mickey's,
that the bread of our communion will be proffered by ATM
and the wine quaffed without taint of sulfites
or trademark infringement, all of which is certainly true
and yet too pat, too much like shooting mice in a barrel
when there are nastier vermin to contest
and purgatories far worse than Disney's realm of immortal
simulacra suckled at the breast of Lake Buena Vista.
There is, for one, Orlando itself,
Orlando rightly considered, Orlando qua Orlando.
Nobody, anywhere, could honestly propose Orlando
as a fit model for human habitation,
city with the character of a turnpike restroom,
city with the soul of a fast-food establishment,
sanitized and corporatized, homogenous and formulaic.
Orlando is the holy land of the branded and franchised,
Orlando is the Jerusalem of commodified delight,
Orlando, Orlando, so many Orlandos
I commence to feel downright Shakespearean,
but here is no Rosalind to dignify our tale,
no Touchstone to transform its tragedy to farce,
because Orlando is the Florida I fear to conceive,
Florida ordained like the antechamber to that afterworld
where jackal-headed Anubis prepares his embalmer's instruments
to pump our veins with tincture of liquid sunshine
until we are reduced to somnambulant acquiescence,
a citizenry mummified within the cambric of material satiety,

within the gated stucco walls of economic segregation
and the hairy stucco arms of Armed Response security,
a people determined to rev our outboards and troll for bass
in the shadow of the form-glass temples to corporate profit
while the fill ponds grow heavy with duckweed and algae
and the golf courses burn with viridian fire
through seasons of rain and seasons of drought
and the metropolis spreads ever outward the bland picnic blankets
of its asphalt dominion, landscape drained of spontaneity and glee,
bones boiled free of communal gristle—is it any wonder
the children of this America rise up with guns
to wreak a senseless vengeance,
the very children that might have saved us,
the ones we had relied on to assemble in fellowship
and attend to councils of greater wisdom
than those to which we have given credence?
Perhaps the children were absent from school the day
these lessons were offered or perhaps
the lessons have been censored from the curriculum
or there was no curriculum or the schools
had been demolished to make room for the future,
a serial cataclysm of vinyl and asphalt,
a republic of bananas and Banana Republics,
where cars are the chosen and credit cards the elect,
where Judge Judy balances the Scales of Justice
and the anthem of our freedom is sung by Chuck E. Cheese.
Here I may testify with absolute conviction:
Chuck E. Cheese is the monstrous embodiment of a nightmare,
the bewhiskered Mephistopheles of ringtoss,
the vampire of our transcendent ideals.
Every Chuck E. Cheese's erected across the mall-lands of America
is another nail in the coffin of human aspiration
and every hour spent in one takes six months off your life.

No, no, no, it's not a theme restaurant or family amusement center
but a vision of infernal despair enjoined in plastic flames,
the clownish horror of the place is unspeakable,
yet I feel that I must speak of it, for I have been
to the birthday party of Emily, turning five,
the birthday party of Max, turning eight or nine,
of Max again, of David and Doris, of Myrna and Roberto,
I can bear witness to its odors of chocolate milk and floor cleanser,
the Formica falsity of its processed cheesefood pseudopizza,
its banquet tables arrayed with pitchers of lurid orange soda
and the kids in the arcade room playing air hockey
and whack-a-mole and teaching one another to cheat at Skee-Ball
to win a screel of coupons to redeem for tiny, chintzy prizes,
the worst sorts of craftily packaged trash—stringless
army parachute guys, malformed monster finger puppets,
Chinese yoyos that self-destruct at the flip of a wrist—
a rainbow-colored peep show designed to entice the youngest
     among us
to invest their lives in a cycle of competitive consumption
and then the animatronic hoedown commences its banjo jangle,
the hairy rodent orchestra chirring their cymbals onstage
as the gray rat-man emerges from his curtain redolent of mildew,
the incubus, the secret sharer, Chuck E. Cheese himself,
and the baby children scream in dismay and the larger children
gag with disinterest and the parents pay no attention at all
while employees with the fear- and candy-glazed eyeballs
of medium-security inmates stutter their pre-scripted remarks
over a public address system in whose interstitial silences
one may discern the voices of the lost upraised in prayer.

     We're having a great day at Chuck E. Cheese—
       Hear us, help us, grant us benison,

Pick up your food at the counter PJ—
    Comfort and guide us, lead us to salvation,
Everyone loves family fun at Chuck E.—
    Bestow the mercies of your blessing
Cheese for your safety wear shoes at all times—
    Upon our souls, we beseech Thee,
Last call for pickup PJ last call—
    Lord of our fathers, Almighty God.

NAGASAKI, UNCLE WALT, THE ESCHATOLOGY OF AMERICA'S CENTURY

Like all good stories it starts with a bang: August 6, 1945.
Little Boy, Oppenheimer's aleph, Hiroshima, the bomb.
America's Century begins in fire and ends,
like any respectable act of creation, in something
resembling ash, Alamogordo to Ragnarok, Genesis
to Nagasaki, the black rain wherein we are forever united
with those whose bones we jellied to magma,
siblings minutely differentiated by the fact
that what the burgeoning clouds bequeathed to us
was not death but Oldsmobiles and wall-to-wall shag,
family sitcoms, Rock Hudson melodramas,
Quisp and Quake and Shake 'n Bake. I'm talking about m-m-
my generation, boomers and boomlets and Watergate babies,
vassals of Dumbo, victims of disco, Disney's demented
suburban spawn held in thrall by Herbie the Love Bug
and Dan'l Boone and frozen dinners in the family room.
For his is the land of Salisbury steak and crinkle-cut fries,
his the encampment holding hostage our dreams,
his the painted desert toward which an ever younger legion
flies to fight and die willingly among the ruins
littered with no plastic cactus. Poor, lost Los Angeles.
Fifty years since the war invented the automobile and it
keeps spreading like an oil slick or fungus,
some deviant flora or insect brood corrupt with radiation,
the *Things* and *Its* our fear became those first flush years
of the Atomic Age. Amazing, this vista, the miles we've logged
from the very first split-levels and miracle appliances,
Levittown to Orange County, the mouse-eared multitude
inching into adolescence as the great consensus waned,
Perry Como supplanted by Elvis, Route 66 replaced by I-40,

Interstates invented by Ike to match the autobahns
he bombed to rubble. And the '60s were born with a whole
lot of shaking and died in the trip wires of Tet,
the '70s churned in a funky inferno—*burn, baby, burn*—
lost souls in sandals and government scandals
preempting the *Brady Bunch* and *Partridge Family*,
and soon they'll be enshrining the '80s
like the happy daze of the '50s before them
as a fun-loving decade of armed intervention and capital gains
overseen by a firm but avuncular Cold Warrior,
a smiling Sandman smelting our stolen ideals to slag.
Burn, baby. Burn. But what will we do for entertainment
now that Uncle Walt is gone, Elvis has left the building,
even the Commies have thrown in the towel?
Where can we turn for self-definition if *Lookinglass* has landed,
Iron Felix fallen, the Titan of the Carpathians
crumbled to chalk on the Victory of Socialism Boulevard?
We've invested so much in World War III it seems a shame
to miss it, killer satellites and high-tech graphics
to grid the incoming contrails, feral survivors
roaming the wasteland in jacked-up desert dune buggies.
For those reared in the shadow of the Fat Man
anything less than global thermonuclear destruction
seems laughable, wimpy, unrealistically naive.
I couldn't begin to count the versions of Armageddon
cast up like driftwood on the shallow bar of my youth:
gamma waves and bacterial plagues, deep-space visitations,
killer rabbits run amok in *Night of the Lepus*.
No screenplay apocalypse, no scenario for world holocaust
could fail to provide me with suitable amusement.
The greenhouse effect? Let's grow oranges in Alaska!
Nuclear winter? We'll wear fur coats!
How many Saturdays did I roam the solitude of Rock Creek Park

whacking the heads from the carpet of May apples
that rose like miniature mushroom people from the loam each
    spring,
the last man left alive, alone with my trusty radio,
stockpiled SpaghettiOs, and Raquel Welch in her mink bikini.
My favorite survivalist parable was that classic of the genre,
The Omega Man: Charlton Heston as a macho scientist
marooned in a barbed-wire penthouse bastion
while the devious albino minions of Brother Matthias essay
to toast him like a cheese puff with their flaming catapult.
To a battalion of prepubescent fifth-grade boys
assembled on my birthday for pizza and then a movie
at the military hospital where my father saw patients
its peculiar logic was irresistible—wandering the streets
of the virus-riddled city, submachine gun in hand,
torching the cowled and cowering enemy, looting at will
from abandoned stores in a consumerist fantasy spree.
Even the recovering soldiers back from Hue and Da Nang
napalmed hairless as rubber lobsters strolling the lobby
in mint-green sanitary gowns during intermission
couldn't dim our heroic bloodlust. Eventually, of course,
the bad guys contrive to harpoon unlucky Charlton
in a fountain, Ahab and the whale rolled into one,
his blood embodying a second chance for the hippie kids
who must repopulate the planet, a vaccine in the sacristy,
a red sea he might have parted against Pharaoh
in a more familiar role, but it isn't that easy this time, Moses,
I mean Chuck, for we have met the enemy and they
seem more than a little familiar. Surprise! It's us.
You and me and Charlton Heston. As climaxes go,
this is a serviceable, if moralistic, warhorse,
an invocation of divine reckoning gaveled from on high
by the supreme arbiter of truth and justice who remains,

for contractual reasons, off camera. For our purposes
such traditional iconography is entirely unsuited.
We must don the body armor of secular materialism
to probe the minefields of the Age of Relativity,
though still our animist soul peeks through
in the totem bulls and bears of Wall Street,
the buffalo at Fermilab, the mustangs at Las Colinas,
the way water draws us from the parched interior
to cluster in postmetropolitan conurbations
gridlocked at the edge of the Great Lakes and oceans.
Isn't this another possible ending, a slam-bang finale
for the movie our search for existential meaning has become,
the gathering-together-of-the-folk-on-the-beach,
a millennial hootenanny of ludic glee, a redemptive conclave
where the blinds and baffles that divide us wash away
while the mother ship announces its queenly ascension
from its secret UFO base beneath the Bermuda Triangle
with the sis-boom-bah anthem of universal kinship?
But does anyone remember the words to that chestnut?
And if we take the sea as our symbol for spiritual longing
have we reduced the human comedy to a beach party flick,
spring break in Fort Lauderdale with Frankie and Annette,
Elvis on board for the making of *Fun in Acapulco*?
Is the theme of salvation even faithful to the script?
Is today's viewing audience likely to credit the trope
of an unseen Canaan on a Hollywood backlot
toward which Chuck Heston would lead us?
We could close with a medley of our greatest hits,
Hula-Hoops to Indian bingo, pinball machines and mechanical
        hearts,
protest rallies, rocket launches, traffic jams, swap meets.
But montage is a throwback to the golden age of Tinseltown,
and we've seen those cheesy newsreels a thousand times.

Our final act should be caged in a more contemporary idiom,
sure, postmodern, postindustrial, post-Ford, Post Toasties,
a mise-en-scène more in keeping with the zeitgeist,
the end-of-the-millennium implication of closure
which could lead us on a journey to the great hereafter,
the wild blue yonder, the sweet by-and-by,
heaven and hell rolled into one brazenly illumined limbo,
the collective *purgatorio* of America's Century,
where the spirits of the departed compose a fluid societal matrix
embracing freedom of expression and laissez-faire economics,
democratic, nonsectarian, centrally air-conditioned,
lacking only a sense of higher purpose—altruism, *civitas,*
the numinous, the sacred—an eternal Las Vegas of the soul,
complete with keno parlors and fast-food franchises,
laundromats and mobile homes and glassy office parks,
a necropolis populated with lonely souls of all descriptions
drinking 7-Eleven coffee on the way to work,
a mosaic we could tile with the pearl and ebony tesserae
of our favorite cultural icons, JFK and LBJ,
Lucy Ricardo and Charlie Parker, Malcolm X
teaching self-empowerment at the local community college,
Speed Racer hunkered down in the grease pit at Jiffy Lube,
John Belushi playing the slots, Sylvia Plath perambulating Wal-Mart
for jumbo packs of Pampers, the self-destroying angels,
we could make a suburb of their deaths: the Blue Deuce Lounge,
where Hank Williams and Janis Joplin torch a plaintive duet
while Marilyn and James Dean slow dance in the dark;
Kerouac's Bar & Grill; Anne Sexton's Brake & Muffler;
Jarrell & O'Hara's Body Shop and Custom Re-
Finishing—Jackson Pollock is out back right now
airbrushing Chinese dragons on a baby-blue conversion van.
We could borrow that van and cruise the Strip at twilight
with all the beautiful, lost, 27-year-old rock and rollers,

Morrison and Hendrix, Buddy Holly and the rest,
the vomit-choked, the chopper-spavined, the shot-down-in-flames.
We could drive the linear palm-lined boulevards
among the immaculate golf courses and planned communities'
manicured lawns, pastel intaglio wavering at poolside,
TVs dreaming of snow in the darkened living rooms.
We could enter the arc-lit freeway slipstream
and climb the desolate escarpments to the higher desert.
We could travel for miles before stopping by the side of the road,
to stretch our legs, and walk out among the Joshua trees
the suicides are lucky enough to become. At the edge
of the plateau, before looking down at the city
sprawled like a uranium nebula in its inhospitable cradle,
we could pause. We could wait there, hands in pockets,
engine running, with the veiled fire flooding over the rise to etch,
among the creosote and sage, a kind of frenzied hieroglyphic,
the projection of a vast, untranslatable energy
against the furrows of dust as pale and frangible as ash.

GUNS N' ROSES

i.m. Tim Dwight, 1958–1994

Not a mea culpa, not an apology, but an admission:
there are three minutes in the middle of "Sweet Child O' Mine"
that still, for all the chopped cotton of the passing years,
for all the muddled victories and defeats of a lifetime,
for all the grief and madness and idiocy of our days,
slay me, just slay me. They sound like how it felt to be alive
at that instant, how it was to walk the streets of Manhattan
in that era of caviar and kill-hungry feedback,
the Big Apple so candy-coated with moral slush and easy money
even the corporate heavyweights could fashion no defense
against decay, all the homeless encamped over cold coffee
at Dunkin' Donuts on upper Broadway, even McDonald's
become a refugee camp for victims of the unacknowledged war
fought beneath the giddy banners of corporatization
as the decade spun down its drain of self-delusion. Where
do we go, where do we go, where do we go
now? What a glorious passage, a shimmering bridge
embodying everything rock and roll aspires to be,
heroic and violent and joyous and juvenile
and throbbing with self-importance and percolating
with melodrama and thrilled and scared by
its own anthemic power, by the kid-on-a-scooter freedom
and the hill a lot steeper than it seemed at first glance,
what the hell, rust never sleeps, live and let die, etc., etc.
And whenever I hear that song, become, now,
a classic of the genre, even as it suffuses me with nostalgia
for those days of malt liquor and BBQ chips,
it gives me cause to think of Axl Rose in his purgatory
self-assembled from paranoia and Malibu chaparral,
wrestling exotic demons, kickboxing with Jesus,
binding and gagging his women with duct tape in the closet,
much the way the heavy metal mentality of the times

seized and militarized his music, sonic warriors
blasting "Paradise City" at the Panamanian dictator,
"Welcome to the Jungle" for the Waco cultists,
Slash and Axl circling the globe, leveling ancient civilizations
with power chords and teenage emotions,
from the Halls of Mentholyptus to the Shores of MTV.
And if Axl appears almost Nixonian in his anguish,
at least he is not Kurt Cobain, forsaken and baby-faced
as J. Michael Pollard in the episode of *Lost in Space*
where Penny goes through the mirror to a realm
of demoniacal toys and that metaphysical bear-monster,
cousin to the troglodytes that chased Raquel Welch
up the cavern tree in *One Million Years B.C.,*
death in its many B-movie guises, so much gaudier
than the killers that walked the streets among us,
the needle and the dollar, the gun and the rose,
and the last time we saw Tim, at Bruce's place
in the Hollywood hills, he recalled the first time
we'd all hung out together in New York, Halloween, 1985,
provincial immigrants tossing back bourbon and tequila,
Tim holding a bundle of Ecstasy for some dealer—
a drug I'd never even heard of—which instead of trying to market
he handed around with cavalier generosity,
packets of powder doused in the tall cans of Colt 45
we drank as we walked the streets of the Village
amid the disintegrating drifts and dregs of the parade,
and finally a midnight show at the Ritz, some L.A. bands
the girls adored done up in black-light fluorescents,
dancing and stage-diving, jubilant and hallucinatory,
getting home somehow on a subway serviced
by orange-vested trolls before waking to cold sweat
and hangover candy and a day of recuperation and the desire
to do it all again. Because there was plenty of time,

we knew, or thought we knew, or were simply too stupid
not to know we didn't know at all, time to waste or kill
before the crashes and commitments that would doom or save
or cast us back into the tide pools of the westering continent.
Tim was still laughing, hauntingly frail, but what I thought
looking out across the canyon was how badly
Los Angeles had aged, wanton and careworn,
like a faded child star sickled with cosmetic surgery scars
still dreaming of a comeback, still scheming and groveling,
as if to prove that nothing really dies in America
but is merely removed from the shelves for repackaging,
coming back crisper and crunchier, cholesterol-free,
as even Axl Rose is coming back with Tommy Stinson on bass
and a sideman wearing a KFC bucket like a Spartan helmet,
and I wish that I could lay the blame for Axl's fucked-up life
on the feral orphanhood of the Pax Atomica,
the alienation of lives begun with no expectation of completion,
it would be simpler that way, for all of us,
but the world did not end in a vortex of toxic fire,
the flying fortresses have returned from the stratosphere
and the missiles endure their nightmares mutely in dark silos
and we have no excuse but the arrogance of power for our narcissism
and no solace but the merciless amplitude of our din.
And that was it, the moment had passed,
another gem or tear for the cut-glass diadem of passing years.
Someone cranked the music up, someone made a toast
to the pool lights and glitter. And then the Pixies
begin some riff-rife, fully surfable rifle shot of a theme song
announcing the ironic revival of our childhood
swaggering like Tony the Tiger atop a station wagon
at an Esso station in 1964, Tony the Tiger
back from the dead, eldritch and transcendent—
rise, the immortals!—

rise to grasp the silver handles
of the casket in procession before us, Ultraman
and Astroboy and Mr. Clean and the Man from Glad
and Josie and the Pussycats
on the Rose Bowl float with their God
Bless America batons atwirl
and then—
huh—
cue the horns,
take it down, break it all apart
and start from nothing to garb our nakedness
with sheets of beaten gold,
cozen us with grieving blossoms,
anoint us with honey in the dry riverbed,
and tell me,
O great devourer,
O master of thorns and ashes,
where do we go
now?

SEPTEMBER 11

1.

Morning, stretching sore muscles on the floor by the bed,
sifting the night's quota of thoughts, images, tasks,
half-remembered insights, odd lines of poetry stranded

by the ebb and flow of the mind. So it is an ocean,
then, this Sea of Consciousness
mitigating, filtering, accommodating everything?

A child's unfinished alphabet puzzle on the sunporch
overlooking the reconfigured beach after the hurricane,
the beyond-dazzling shimmer of light across water.

Twenty-six letters, *a* to *z*, fingerable, adept.
Is it possible to intuit from these simplistic characters
Leaves of Grass, the *Duino Elegies*?

Who, shown a hydrogen molecule, would envision the sun?
As from leaf to rain forest, as from ant to biosphere,
as from a single brick to imagine Manhattan,

as from a human instant the totality of a life,
of lives interwoven, families and affiliations,
the time-trawled nets of societies and cultures.

So the arc of creativity is an ungrounded rainbow,
and cause for hope. Why distrust the universe?
We are engines burning violently toward the silence.

2.

Frigate birds in high wind over the inlet, enormous chains
of the construction cranes rattling like rusty wind chimes,
current running hard out through the channel,

schools of quick minnows along the rocks while midstream
the big fish wait for a meal, silver-gray flashes
of their torpedoing bodies—tarpon, bluefish, snook.

Heaps of seaweed on the beach, rim of clouds on the horizon
to mark the trailing edge of the storm pinwheeling
north to ravage the Carolinas, while along the jetty

Cuban fishermen with cruciform tattoos
are hand-netting baitfish to dump in old roofing buckets
like needling rain or schools of silver punctuation marks,

liquid semicolons seething in paratactic contortions,
prisoners seeking to deny a period to their sentence.
Surfers by the dozen—this is what they live for,

the cyclonic surge—waxing their boards,
paddling out, rising and tumbling.
Three fish on the sand, Jackson says they are cowfish,

one still breathing, we throw it back.
A few other families picking through the flotsam,
eelgrass, purplish crenellated whelks,

a brittle-shelled starfish,
his little polyp feelers probing our palms,
estrella de mar, estrellita,

butterflies lit by chimerical sunlight on orange-fingered
sea fern fronds, the smooth black coral trees
we use as Halloween decorations,

tubular mangrove seeds, coconuts and buoys,
blue and yellow tops of soda bottles,
pink cigarette lighters, a toothbrush, a headless doll.

3.

That they were called *towers,* the irony of that
ancient fortress word, twin strongholds, twin keeps,
that they fell and the day was consumed

in smoke of their ruination, in dust and ashen iota.
And the next day came and still the towers were fallen.
That morning I went for a long, aimless walk

along the beach, listening to *Blonde on Blonde,*
watching the sunlight stroke and calibrate the waves
like the silvery desire in Dylan's voice

as the skipped heartbeat cymbals declared closure.
Later I met the gods emerging from a topaz-faceted sea,
their long hair flashing in the wind,

and the gods were beautiful, bold, and young,
and one called out to me as they arose and came forth.
Come and see the world we have created

from your suffering. And I beheld a city
where blood ran through streets the color of raw liver,
stench of offal and kerosene and torched flesh,

tongueless heads impaled on poles and severed limbs
strung on barbed wire beneath unresting surveillance cameras,
industrial elevators shuttling bodies to the furnace rooms,

and speakers blaring incongruous slogans, the tinkle of a toy piano,
maudlin and inane, and vast movie screens depicting
the glittering eyeballs of iron-masked giants,

and beyond the city hills of thorn trees and people in shanties
talking softly, awaiting their time in the carnage below.
No, no, laughed the god. *That is your world,*

the world we created is here—.
And I saw rolling hills carpeted in wildflowers,
tall grasses swaying in the wind,

no trees, no streams,
just grass and wind and endless light.
These fields are watered with human tears.

4.

Images of the aftermath: smoke and rubble,
gothic spire of a wall still standing, ash-white paper
blizzards of notary calculation like the clay tablets

of the Sumerians smashed and abandoned.
They seem, now, already, distant and historicized,
like Matthew Brady's Civil War photographs—

the dead sniper at Little Round Top, the Devil's Den,
blasted fields and ravaged orchards of the homeland.
And the camps of the Union Army,

numberless crates of supplies at the quartermaster's depot,
acres of wagon teams like the truckers
hauling debris away from Ground Zero, how Whitman

would have lauded their patriotic industry,
carting the wreckage of empire,
as he praised the young soldiers in their valor,

"genuine of the soil, of darlings and true heirs,"
as he cared for them in the army hospitals in Washington,
bringing to the wounded small, homely comforts—

apples, tobacco, newspapers, string,
pickles and licorice and horehound candy,
pocket change to buy a drink from the dairywoman

peddling fresh milk cot to cot in the field wards,
a comb, a book, a bowl of rice pudding
for Henry Boardman of the 27th Connecticut—

the democratic simplicity of his compassion,
whatever the erotic charge of its currency,
whatever its voyeuristic aspect,

discovering in the moment of material attention
the salve for a wounded life, and in the lives of the wounded
a serum for the injured nation. Meaning, by *compassion,*

his unique, coercive, actively embodied brand of empathy,
his conspiratorial love of self and other
intermingled, undivided, prelapsarian and entire,

his kindness, his tenderness,
Walt Whitman's tenderness is everything,
source of his greatness and key to his enigmatic soul,

the agent that calls sentimental platitudes to task
and elevates his grief into lasting eloquence,
the force that disavows anger for love

even amid the inconceivable
carnage of that war, the suffering of those men,
the magnitude of that national trauma.

But *Leaves of Grass* does not negate Gettysburg,
lilacs could not return Lincoln
to a grieving people.

No poem can refute the killing fields.
Art will not stop the death squads
sharpening their machetes in the village square before dawn,

the militiamen, the partisans, the cutters-off of hands,
boy soldiers in new barracks playing dice,
the child nailed to the hawthorn tree and the parents

beyond the barbed wire forced to admire the work of the nailers,
the nails themselves, iron ore and machines to quarry it,
mills and factories, depots and warehouses,

the distribution software,
the brown truck and the deliveryman,
wheelbarrows of lopped hands burned in pits with gasoline,

pretty smiling girls favored by the rape brigades,
the believers, the zealots, sergeants at arms, gangsters,
ethnic cleansers and counterinsurgency units,

tyrants, ideologues, defenders of justice,
technological sentinels in hardened bunkers
scanning infrared monitors for ignition signatures,

mass graves and secret facilities,
scientists chained to the lightning of matter,
the atoms themselves,

neutrinos and quarks, leptons
refracting alpha particles as words reflect
the stolen light of truth or revelation,

the faces of the terrorists as the airplane strikes the tower,
the faces of the firemen ascending the stairwell,
the faces of Stephen Biko's torturers at the amnesty hearing

while the dutiful son listens impassively
as if attending Miltonic lectures on human suffering,
the real, the actual, the earthly, ether of bodily want,

love and its granules pouring from the crucible,
rain to bathe the ingots, a gray horizon of muddy shoals
where oceangoing freighters are taken to pieces

by half-naked laborers wielding hammers and blowtorches,
a wrecking ground reverberating with gong-sounds
and the screams of yielding metal,

black-and-white photographs to document
that place, that labor, human history,
the work of men.

5.

Strange that we are born entire, red-faced and marsupial,
helpless but whole, no chrysalis or transformation
to enlarge or renew us, unless—who is to say that death

might not signify a wing-engendering reanimation
such as believers in the afterlife propose?
Is it a dream, then, this beach of seraphic sunlight,

silos full of clouds, monarch butterflies
flown from Mexico to roost on storm-uprooted trees
as schools of stingrays weave their way

through a realm of water which is their own,
the breaking through, the crossing over,
wing tips in the wave-curl

impinging upon us as ghosts or angels might,
cracks in the crystal spheres through which perfume
floods unending into our world?

Which passes, as lightning or a waning moon
drawn above the Atlantic, my Atlantic,
rose petals poured from silver goblets into molten glass,

nectar of apples and papayas,
shoes composed of wampum and desire,
my own Atlantic—but, why are you laughing?

Not at you, no.
Then with me?
No . . .

Clouds more enormous than souls,
more sacred, fatal, devoted,
saints climbing pearl-inlaid stairs into the burning sky,

saints or golden ants, but no— *No?*
Are you sure? And the god smiled,
and picked up his scythe.

6.

Odor on the breeze of sea foam and decay,
the stars' genuflections,
subsidence, forgetfulness, the tides.

And beneath the still surface,
what depths?
And the creatures in the chasms below the waves?

All night I dreamt of mermaids caught in fishing nets
and now, jeweled with sargassum in the surf,
the body of a mermaid, drowned.

SHOPPING FOR POMEGRANATES
AT WAL-MART ON NEW YEAR'S DAY

Beneath a ten-foot-tall apparition of Frosty the Snowman
with his corncob pipe and jovial, over-eager, button-black eyes,
holding, in my palm, the leathery, wine-colored purse
of a pomegranate, I realize, yet again, that America is a country
about which I understand everything and nothing at all,
that this is life, this ungovernable air
in which the trees rearrange their branches, season after season,
never certain which configuration will bear the optimal yield
of sunlight and water, the enabling balm of nutrients,
that so, too, do Wal-Mart's ferocious sales managers
relentlessly analyze their end-cap placement, product mix,
and shopper demographics, that this is the culture
in all its earnestness and absurdity, that it never rests,
that each day is an eternity and every night is New Year's Eve,
a cavalcade of B-list has-beens entirely unknown to me,
needy comedians and country singers in handsome Stetsons,
sitcom stars of every social trope and ethnic denomination,
pugilists and oligarchs, femmes fatales and anointed virgins
throat-slit in offering to the cannibal throng of Times Square.
Who are these people? I grow old. I lie unsleeping
as confetti falls, ash-girdled, robed in sweat and melancholy,
click-shifting from QVC to reality TV, strings of commercials
for breath freshener, debt reconsolidation, a new car
lacking any whisper of style or grace, like a final fetid gasp
from the lips of a dying Henry Ford, potato-faced actors
impersonating real people with real opinions
offered forth with idiot grins in the yellow, herniated studio light,
actual human beings, actual souls bought too cheaply.
That it never ends, O Lord, that it never ends!
That it is relentless, remorseless, and it is on right now.
That one sees it and sees it but sometimes it sees you, too,
cowering in a corner, transfixed by the crawler for the storm alert,

home videos of faces left dazed by the twister, the car bomb,
the war always beginning or already begun, always
the special report, the inside scoop, the hidden camera
revealing the mechanical lives of the sad, inarticulate people
we have come to know as "celebrities."
Who assigns such value, who chose these craven avatars
if not the miraculous hand of the marketplace
whose torn cuticles and gaudily painted fingernails resemble nothing
so much as our own? Where does the oracle reveal our truths
more vividly than upon that pixilated spirit-glass
unless it is here, in this tabernacle of homely merchandise,
a Copernican model of a money-driven universe
revolving around its golden omphalos, each of us summed
and subtotaled, integers in an equation of need and consumption,
desire and consummation, because Hollywood had it right all along,
the years are a montage of calendar pages and autumn leaves,
sheet music for a nostalgic symphony of which our lives comprise
but single trumpet blasts, single notes in the hullabaloo,
or even less—we are but motes of dust in that atmosphere
shaken by the vibrations of time's imperious crescendo.
That it never ends, O Lord. That it goes on,
without pause or cessation, without pity or remorse.
That we have willed it into existence, dreamed it into being.
That it is our divine monster, our factotum, our scourge.
That I can imagine nothing more beautiful
than to propitiate such a god upon the seeds of my own heart.

Part Five

Poems

WOE

Consider the human capacity for suffering,
our insatiable appetite for woe.
I do not say this lightly
but the sandwiches at Subway
suck. Foaming lettuce,
mayo like rancid bear grease,
meat the color of a dead dog's tongue.
Yet they are consumed
by the millions
and by the tens of millions.
So much for the food. The rest
I must pass over in silence.

THE KEY LIME

Curiously yellow hand grenade
of flavor; Molotov cocktail
for a revolution against the bland.

VICE PRESIDENT OF PANTS

turns out to be my friend Marvin's job title
at a local clothing manufacturer
as I learned from a recent newspaper article
about "victims of the downturn,"

though even after some serious erosion
his paycheck rolls enough biweekly zeros
to belie whatever expectations
you may have harbored about those

who toil in the vineyards of leisurewear,
and I can't help but envy the Director of Kneesocks,
and the Undersecretary of Ascots,
and wonder whether the Alcalde of Guayaberas

might be hiring an assistant sometime soon,
because in all honesty this poetry gig
is like feeding chocolate donuts to a hungry tiger
or planting sunflowers on the moon.

WILD THING

I will be forever nineteen driving a white Impala convertible down
    the Pacific Coast Highway while the radio plays nothing but my
    favorite songs.
I will live among the wild men of Borneo, drink boar's blood, watch
    the slow dance of planets through my bamboo telescope.
I will alter the consciousness of the free world, shake the
    philosophical foundations of Western civilization while dating
    Vanna White.
I will rock the Roxy and the Ritz, ride the rails, roam center field for
    the Cubs.
I will rise and shine, I will reign, I will rule, believe me.
Alas, life is poor preparation for death.
All those years of practice for the grand event that never happens,
no flute recital before the masses, no squash game with God.
In such matters our shortsightedness is fundamental.
History is a wave and we surf it beautifully,
carving the face, shredding the curl of that perfectly marbled breaker
spiced with essential stoke. Or so we imagine.
But before this wave came others, and beyond it lies
a veritable ocean of rills and wavelets and mighty tsunamis
we've failed to notice, our eyes so full of spray,
blinded by the tingling sensations of the moment,
as if time were a force field or energized aura,
a second skin, like gravity or desire,
that by its very nature constricts our vision, contains us
as a pig's intestine stuffed with pork and anise
by some overwrought Italian butcher. How else
could my wife continue to wear those shoes,
those black-buckled high-tops, combat boots for elves,
which will so clearly seem an utter embarrassment
in the photo album twenty years from now.
My god, look what I wore in the '90s!
How else to explain the statue of Ceres atop the Board of Trade,

elegantly appropriate but left without a face, unfinished,
because they didn't think the city would grow tall enough to notice.
And don't we all recognize that blank expression?
Don't we each cherish our unique and individual nature,
every paper cut or broken heart the first, the most severe,
each vow or resolution the mark of some brave new beginning.
No two snowflakes are exactly alike
but every fucking snowflake is pretty much the same,
every life a variation on a theme of suffering and meaninglessness,
full of distractions—frisbees, beautiful trees,
girls in orange sandals—in fact the distractions
are the main event, there is no grace period,
no warm-up tosses or pre-season schedule,
the game has not only begun it's the top of the sixth inning
and you still haven't scored. A shutout.
The world has pitched a shutout against your life.
For all your slick manipulations of that magic bat
you're deep in the hole, the count's against you,
your net result is a fat string of goose eggs
hung like loops of fresh kielbasa from the rafters.
And time is running out, we're into the seventh,
now it's the eighth and the lights are coming on,
the fans are clapping with nervous anticipation.
Look, out in the bullpen, he's warming up:
the main man, the big guy, the stopper, the ace.
But what about those dreams, your hopes for the future—
to plumb the depths of the Marianas Trench in a gilded
    bathysphere,
to write the epic masterwork of greed and heroism and love,
to build a house with your own two hands in the hills outside of
    Santa Fe
and raise up chickens and dogs and a family there,
the Jet Ski, the guitar lessons, the macramé? Hey,

I'd better get serious, get something going before it's too late.
It is too late. Bottom of the ninth. Two gone.
They've given the signal and he's entering the game,
he's coming in to face you, he's making his way slowly across the
    grass.
The inexorable closer is coming, believe me,
it isn't Mitch Williams.

POEM THAT NEEDS NO INTRODUCTION

I.

Listen, I have endured so much bad art in my lifetime
that my brain actually throbs and pulses
in the manner of a 1960s comic-book supervillain
and my skull threatens to burst at the seams like a lychee nut
at the mere thought of all those tuneless bands and lousy etchings
and earnest readings in coffeehouses
smelling of clove cigarettes,
pretentious photos of phallomorphic icebergs,
the opening at the gallery hung with stillborn elephants—
what could you say?—and one unforgettable night
a conceptual dance performance akin to a ritual sacrifice
with the audience as victims—as if art
might prove the literal death of me—all this,
all this and so much more,
only to find myself here, in Bratislava,
at the Ars Poetica poetry festival,
yet again drinking red wine from a plastic cup
while the poets declaim in languages
dense and indecipherable as knotted silk, thinking, well,
what could be better than this?

II.

Perhaps it would be better if the air-conditioning worked
and the keg of Zlatý Bažant had not run dry
but the local wine is unexpectedly delicious, hearty as wild boar's
    blood,
and the very existence of such an exuberantly cacophonous conclave
in this diminutive and innocuous backwater of Mitteleuropa
makes me yearn to do something hearty and wine-soaked and
    boarish—

no, not boorish—to shout spontaneous bebop musings
like the hipster Beatnik poet Fred from Paris
or crack wise like the balding Frank O'Hara imitator from Vienna
or sing like the yodeling, pop-eyed jokester from Prague
or simply intone with great seriousness like the well-mannered poets
from Warsaw and Wrocław, Berlin and Budapest and Brno.

III.

o river sand,
sink deeper and fling yourself
into my whirlpool!

blue sunflower gas-ring octopus—
what brings you
to the rain forest, amigo?

IV.

Well, that came out a bit like Bashō imitating Corso
but the thought is what counts when it is 10:45 and you are drunk
enough to believe a poem scribbled on a festival program
could change the world
and when someone says time is an invisible marauder
I shout *Fuck you!* and everybody smiles.

V.

This poem will change the world.
This poem is a revolutionary anthem to global insurrection.
This poem is an international pop sensation, over twenty million
    sold.

This poem saved the baby from the burning building.
This poem knows how to howl, to hoot like an owl.
This poem refuses to throw in the towel.

This poem is an imposter, down with this poem!
This poem has been weaponized.
I am breathing its evil fumes, its paralytic murk.

This poem twists my arm until I cry uncle.
This poem will never help me no matter how much I beg.
Help me, please, somebody help me!

This poem wants to kick some ass.
This poem is going to mess you up so bad.
This poem will bury you, my friend.

VI.

But this poem really digs your sister, with her pigtails
and her songs about polar bears and fast rides to immortality,
your sister is someone to run away with to live
in a castle in a dark Teutonic forest or a cheap apartment
with no furniture but a futon and typewriter in the city
underneath the city that is underneath this city.

VII.

Take a swig of wine and it is 12:15.
Another and it is ten past two.

Fuck you!

But where was I?
Ah yes, Bratislava.

VIII.

At the Mayor's Palace we are instructed to visit the Apple Festival,
a "new tradition" created by the Ministry of Culture
modeled upon the actual traditions of the Slovak country folk
who feel, one can only assume, quite strongly about their apples.

Try as we might we cannot find any sign of the festival
and when we return to the Ministry of Culture
the woman at the desk denies any knowledge of it.
Not to worry, she says, next week begins the Cabbage Festival.

IX.

And tonight is the big national soccer match
and the exuberant crowd watching on jumbo screens in the square
is drinking Coca-Cola from minuscule aluminum cans provided by
    girls
in red jumpsuits and Afro wigs as a promotion but where was I?

Ah yes, art—art is what we came for and what we got
was a reminder that this is how it begins, no, not in fright wigs
but a communion of scars and charms and midnight plunder,
a reminder that even our most profound individual suffering

amounts to little more than ashes on the grate of a city
engulfed in eternal flames, which is certainly not this charming
metropolis of beer gardens and trolleys and long-haired Slavic
    angels
whose golden swords glitter madly above the Danube at dawn.

X.

Ladies and gentlemen, the bar is now closed.

You've been a wonderful audience
and I want to thank you all
for coming tonight
and to leave you with one last piece,
if I can find the right page, ah yes, here we go.

This is a poem that needs no introduction.

POETRY AND FICTION

Their affair has been tempestuous,
and then some. Like us

they like to get it on,
to rut and hump, bang a gong,

but then grow sullen,
wondering not if but when

the end will come. He says to her:
You're not all pretty flowers

and hippie skirts, bitch!
And she: *If you want to switch*

genres go buy a thesaurus,
don't just mope around all morose

and quasi-narrative. And so it goes.
They criticize each other's clothes,

her eye for art, his ear for music,
then they hit the sack,

and pledge to give it one more chance.
Theirs is a heterotextual romance.

HEMINGWAY DINES ON
BOILED SHRIMP AND BEER

I'm the original two-hearted brawler.
I gnaw the scrawny heads from prawns,
pummel those mute, translucent crustaceans,
wingless hummingbirds, salt-water spawned.
As the Catalonians do, I eat the eyes at once.
My brawny palms flatten their mainstays.
I pop the shells with my thumbs, then crunch.

Just watch me as I swagger and sprawl,
spice-mad and sated, then dabble in lager
before I go strolling for stronger waters
down to Sloppy Joe's. My stride as I stagger
shivers the islands, my fingers troll a thousand keys.
My appetite shakes the rock of the nation.
The force of my miction makes the mighty Gulf Stream.

MAIZEL AT SHORTY'S IN KENDALL

All shift them sugar donuts
been singing to me,
calling to me something crazy in a voice
Dolly Parton'd be proud of—*Maizel, honey,*
eat us up! Like that.
Friendly. Nice and sweet, all
glazed up together in that box, as if they was
happy about being what they
is, surely more than this
jelly-junkie waitress hooked on
Krispy Kremes can say. Halve the moon,
leave a frosted crescent for some other girl.
Maizel, you ain't kidding
no one, honey.
Of a certainty you're gonna eat that yourself,
probably soon's you get these BB-
Q
ribs to them boys at table
sixteen. Nice-looking boys, too.
These days we're getting the,
uh, Cuban mostly,
virtually all what you call Hispanic-speaking.
White folks gone moved up to Broward County, like my
ex. *Maizel, you shut*
your mouth about that man! Sweet Gee-
zus, honey, ain't this ring of sugar gold enough?

WHAT THEY ATE

All manner of fowl and wild game: venison, raccoon, opossum,
    turkey.
Abundant fishes, excepting salmon, which ws. found distasteful.
Meat of all sorts, especially pig, which roamed free and was fatty.
Also shellfish: quahogs and foot-long oysters, lobster, though
    considered wasteful.

Wild fruit: huckle and rasp, blue being known as "skycolored" berries.
Parsnips, turnips, carrots, onions: these sown loosely and rooted out;
while these were cultivated in orchards: apples, peaches, apricots,
    cherries.
Cabbage—favored by the Dutch as *koolslaa,* by the Germans as
    sauerkraut—

was boiled with herbs brought from England: thyme, hyssop,
    marjoram, parsley.
Pumpkin, dried, or mashed with butter, where yams grew sparsely.
Corn, husked with beans as *succotash;* called *samp* when milled to
    grist;
in the South, hulled and broken, as *hominy;* or fried with bacon as
    grits.
Maple ws. not favored; loaves of white sugar worth considerable
    money
were kept under lock, cut with special sugar shears. For honey,

bees were imported, called "English flies" by the Narragansett.

CAPITALIST POEM #36

We've got this cheese down here to give away,
tens of thousands of pounds of cheese.

We're trying to establish procedures and specifications,
rules to discourage speculation and hoarding,

guidelines to foster the proper use of this
extraordinary resource. What we need is a system.

I mean it. Not one damn piece of cheese
leaves here until we get this thing figured out.

ODE TO BUREAUCRATS

> *I cherish tongs*
> *and scissors.*

—PABLO NERUDA, "ODE TO THINGS"

Practitioners of oblivion, signatories
of arcane regret
without whose seal we may not enter
into paradise appropriately
entailed,
fated duty, the onus
of their diligence,
the layers of it,
sanctified and sacrificial,
rheum
of pallid eyeballs
immured
in fluorescent cubicles,
municipal camouflage
of coffee rings
and uniform collars,
vestibules of onionskin,
reams and sheets
and terminals,
inkless stick pens
chained to gouged linoleum
as if to strike blood from a twig,
their codes and initials and #2 bubbles,
verification and secondary verification,
their official contrition,
their sorrow, for
there is nothing to be done,
the renewal date has passed,

the balance is insufficient,
the identification numbers do not match,
the procedure is not covered,
the check is in the mail,
the scissors you ordered have arrived
in your office
and they are blunt and monstrous
as the bill of a stork
gone mad
in mating season,
scissors an irascible child might have fashioned
from humble elements
as a plaything,
hinged flanges forged
from metal too weak to whet or hone
bloodied by thumbs
razored
on ragged iron finger-rings,
low-bid scissors
procured by central purchasing,
scissors only the immortal
Chairman could love,
cheap scissors, bad scissors, apocalyptic scissors,
these are your scissors,
Mr. McGrath,
sign here,
please, front and back,
in triplicate.

BECAUSE THIS IS FLORIDA

Because this is Florida, we can be what we choose to be,
say, Dixie-fried Cubano rednecks. It's that kind of place.
When the heavy metal band plays "Rocky Top, Tennessee"

they all stomp and sing along—I should say *we*
sing along, at the annual State Fair, a very weird place.
Because this is Florida, I feel like an anomaly,

but the truth of it is I'm them and they're me,
and now we're stamping and hooting all over the place
while the Texas swing band plays "Rocky Top, Tennessee"

and Haitian kids dip kettle candy beneath a live oak tree
in historic "Cracker Country," apt and ironic misnomer for the place,
because this is Florida, after all, not Texas or Tennessee.

Florida, Florida. At times I can't believe what I see
and don't know how to feel about living in a place
where a bluegrass fiddler plays "Rocky Top, Tennessee"

while Rome burns. Is it just me, or an epidemic of mistaken identity,
the state of confusion that plagues this sun-bedeviled place?
Because this is Florida, I beg you to believe me,
the steel drum band from Trinidad plays "Rocky Top, Tennessee."

VILLANELLE

Bouncing along like a punch-drunk bell,
its Provençal shoes too tight for English feet,
the villanelle is a form from hell.

Balletic as a tapir, strong as a gazelle,
strict rhyme and formal meter keep a beat
as tiresome as a punch-drunk bell-

hop talking hip hop at the IHOP—*no substitutions
on menu items, no fries with the chimichanga,
no extra syrup*—what the hell

was that? Where did my rhyme go—uh, compel—
almost missed it again, damn, can you feel the heat
coming off this sucker? Red hot! *Ding!* (Sound of a bell.)

Hey, do I look like a busboy to you, like an el-
evator operator, like a trained monkey or a parakeet
singing in my cage? Get the hell

out of the Poetry Hotel!
defeat mesquite tis mete repeat
Bouncing along like a punch-drunk bell,
the villanelle is a form from—*Write* it!—hell.

JAMES WRIGHT, RICHARD HUGO, THE VANISHING FORESTS OF THE PACIFIC NORTHWEST

At least they died of smoke and age and not some awful, active form
of suicide. To keep sight of the forest for love of the suffering trees;
to damp the black or bitter ashes; not to surrender one's humanity
to callousness or grief: this is the hard part. There was much
    hardness
in their lives but no bitterness so terrible that what remained
seemed not worth having, no fatal poison in their pure American

wellspring. Where did they find such faith? How could America
retain its luster in eyes familiar with exile and war, the informal
inequalities of the factory floor? Why do the bleached remains
of Montana farms assume the character of barren cottonwood trees,
equal testament to the harshness of the local winter and the hardiness
of the will to endure, what Hollywood likes to call "the human

spirit," though why confine such a universal instinct to humanity?
Why believe it's we alone who suffer? How can the native American
ash and alder and Sitka spruce not possess some inkling of the
    harsh
truth when serpentine logging roads and clear-cut scars form
the totem shapes of grizzly paws on slopes bereft of trees,
when of the great, fog-shouldered forest so little still remains?

Or does it? In Broadway stalls I've seen their work remaindered,
cut-rate and still unsold, disregarded by the very people
they spent their lives extolling, and yet there is more in their poetry
than the ghost of the trees killed for paper. There is more to
    America
than wastefulness and greed and abuse, which are merely forms
of our inherent human weakness, manifestations of the hardship

we suffer when forced to choose for ourselves. Freedom is a hard
row to hoe, our cross to bear, individually and with whatever
     remnant
of communal will remains to us, whatever common vision yet
     informs
our deepest dreams and beliefs, the solitary will or the deeply
     human
dream of community, this central paradox, so typically American,
between the good of the wood and the rights of individual trees.

For me, they loom like redwoods or Douglas fir, the last big trees
of the endangered forest. The timbre of their voices, their wounded
     hearts
still large enough for sugar beets and four-door Buicks, all things
     American,
all things of simple dignity. Alone or gathered at the river, what
     remains
is the democratic song, their rich, vernacular empathy with the
     people,
a common thread of praise. Jim and Dick, in keeping with this form

I carve your informal names in a Western red cedar, totem-pole tree
of the original Americans, because it is sacred and strong of heart.
What thou lovest well remains distinctly, triumphantly human.

ALLEN GINSBERG

I met him only once, at a party in Vinnie Katz's old apartment
    above a Thai restaurant on 55th Street in Chicago, spring of
    1983 or '84.
Earlier that evening he gave a reading at the university, finger
    cymbals, ashram chanting, not as much of the early ecstatic
    genius as had been hoped,
not the majestic anguish of "Howl" but a serious performance
    nonetheless, warmly greeted by an audience of many hundreds.
It seemed even more crowded at the party, where Vinnie's band, the
    Throbbers, a loose-jointed, Velvets-inspired power trio,
rattled the walls of the linoleum-tiled kitchen as we did our usual
    thing, menthol cigarettes and aggressive dancing,
cheap liquor sloshed from aluminum ashtrays, a lot of ironic social
    commentary on secondhand couches smelling of smoke and cat
    piss.
Ginsberg sat hunched in a back room, Buddha-like, holding court;
    the omnisexual dimension of his Socratic shtick was a bit
    unnerving,
even worse was the way Peter Orlovsky would flick the tip of my
    nose with his finger as I posed burning questions like *Why did*
    Kerouac have to die, man?
He seemed tired, sure, how many times had he been through this
    routine, how many earnest young poets dreaming of glory,
looking for wisdom or validation or whatever, how many dim
    bohemian scenes edging toward ash-blistered dawn,
but his patience never faltered, his tipsy smile, he never sold out the
    night or the life or the art that counted him as a bead on its
    prayer-string.
And then it was dawn, or something like it, near dawn, Chicago—
    though it could have been New York, Denver, San Francisco,
the American city in all its splendid yearning to be lost and longing
    to belong, its sidewalks of dog shit and sparkling mica,

a train passing over the viaduct, the embankment spectral with
   waif-paper and what I took to be ghost-weeds trembling in the
   vinegar light.
Not weeds but coarse flowers risen from the pavement. Not ghosts
   but souls seeking voices to greet the dawn.

PAX ATOMICA TRIPTYCH

From the imperium, eyeless, tongueless,
to witness, to taste. . . . From the uranium cradle to hear
hosannas ascend from the ashes of rung bells. . . .

Adam and Eve: 1969

"(Sittin' on) The Dock of the Bay" is everywhere that year,
humming from the radio of the old blue Chevy
at the brand-new drive-thru bank off Metzerott Road where

you'd get a purple lollipop from the lady if you were lucky.
And then Otis Redding died in the plane wreck,
or he already had, and that knowledge is bared to a child's scrutiny,

and the keen of it enhances the soundtrack,
grief and joy, each a movement, each a groove, each
a tone to be borne and abided, rueful and honey-struck

as the untroubled melancholy of his voice.
And then the assassination of Martin Luther King,
first glimmer of the ways in which

the melody's ampersand ensnares us, first inkling
of the intertwined harmony of self and society,
call and response, part and counterpart sung

in the choral grandiloquence of the common polity
while the grave-robbers torching oblivion
comment more eloquently than any thin-tied anchor on TV,

my father's commute to the city dogged by the contagion
of Georgia Avenue storefronts looted to cinders.
And then my best friend's father sent off to Vietnam—

we were still, marginally, military; Sunday dinner
at the Officers' Club—and the inverse celebration
when my uncle Billy pulled a lucky draft number.

He was my favorite babysitter, ballplayer, the one
who took me to the drive-in to see
the double feature that poured a mythological foundation

for my adolescence—*The Good, the Bad and the Ugly,*
followed by *One Million Years* B.C.
Clint Eastwood and Raquel Welch as Adam and Eve,

ideal gender models, everything we desired and desired to be.
How could I have known the years it takes to unlearn
certain lessons, singing "Sugar, Sugar" with the Archies

in the backseat while the honeycomb of our innocence burned
in the streets, everything we would inherit
cast and scorified in the crucible of those years?

How could I tell what was real from what was not?
When Raquel pawed her caveman I smiled,
when Clint said draw I shot.

Iowa: 1983

First trip alone across the country: a dream of driving
through driving rain in Iowa, sodden Iowa,
miles of drenched earth passed through in the gloaming,

roads of pickup trucks, hogpens, corn bins, silos,
a grocery where I stop for apples and white bread,
streetlights reflected on asphalt and dented iron,

on a bright orange Subaru I acknowledge with a nod
as I acknowledge myself, behind the wheel,
Woody Guthrie and the Ramones, the open road,

all that, the scope of the world, its gravity and zeal
beyond rain-wet windows, its diverse
and circumstantial passage, even the familiar become unreal

in light of that unscrolling: taste of liverwurst
and sweet-pickle sandwiches; tears of a woman
on a pay phone beside a piebald horse

in some city flashing past, gone,
perhaps Cedar Rapids; atavistic vision of deepest greenness,
the summoning sheen and wavelength of the corn,

as if the kernels radiated an oceanic luminescence
the husks worked to cocoon and sequester
back into the dark. Of course it was

all much stranger than that, richer and sadder
in its unique and particular word-defying actuality
than my familiar penciled grid of sequential semesters.

Different how, in what way? I can't say.
I mean that it is unsayable, a string of precious shells
or trading beads—*cow, brook, hay*—

not the coinage of names but the things themselves,
their totality, their scale and dimension,
the knowledge that there are spheres and levels

one has never conceived: so this is what the rain
feels like in Iowa, in California; this is another way,
another state, another life, another vision.

And then what? What to equal that revelatory awe?
Elizabeth's beauty like an exhibition
of blown-glass roses, her heart's raw glory,

the birth of our children,
that great awakening, leaving the hospital
our first morning together like a vestal procession

passing from the lobby into the lightfall
of a pure blue Chicago spring
as if crossing some threshold of universal

import, powered by mysterious agency, a door opening
silently as the future opens its automatic portal
before us, second by second, invisible and astonishing.

My son is born and I am no longer immortal.
The ring shall be closed, the cycle fulfilled.
I am bound over, as in a fairy tale,

to the will of time, pledged to this world
by an oath of fearful enchantment.
Pledged. Promised. Bound over. Beguiled.

Everybody Knows John Lennon Is Dead: 2004

Seated on the avenue eating almond ice cream beneath the orange trees
the Andalusian heat seems at last to have lessened, or
at least there is a breeze to squall the dusty citrus leaves

along the cobbled alleyways as a mélange of ambient music emerges
from the barrio—Eurodisco, Hendrix and the Beatles,
flamenco guitar. A kid on a Vespa hops the curb to deliver

a serrano ham to the bar across the street,
joint of a pig wrapped in muslin carried crosstown
on his shoulder. Nice to know they still resist our microbial foibles,

our fetish with sterility, though there are clearly some
exotic new strains of growth in Sevilla's petri dish.
You can tell how much has changed by the Germans begowned

in halter tops and spandex shorts milling in fiendish
prolixity around a cathedral that resembles a reticulated spider
escaped from some dank cage of the Iberian Dark Age. As if

every least rain droplet of the future were not equally and
    altogether
new, alike as minted coins or the waters of the fountain before La
    Giralda
toward which even now the carriage horses stare in mute desire.

Strange the way one's life comes to seem a historical diorama,
looking back as from rocky peaks across golden valleys
where regiments of moonlit sunflowers lay siege to the Alhambra.

Sometimes, in the childhood of a now past century,
my family would forgo dinner to banquet on banana splits
at the old Gifford's ice cream parlor out the parkway,

with the ornate water fountain and marble tabletops,
cloth napkins and fluted silver spoons and formal glassware,
as here, though this, however reminiscent, is not

American ice cream. You can tell by the intensity of flavor,
the almondness of the almond, as you can tell from the woven
     rubber
chairs that this is not my long-gone suburbia, or any American
     anywhere,

though it could perhaps be Rome, thirty years ago, when the street
     vendors
hawked necklaces of hammered iron nails wired to leather thongs
and those clickety-clackety plastic bolas in the floodlights along the
     Tiber,

a city of bridges and diesel fumes and casual decay, like this one,
though you can tell it isn't Rome by the scent of rotten citrus in the
     air,
and the muzzled shadows of Moorish arches, and the wine is wrong,

and though it is always childhood for somebody, somewhere,
it certainly isn't mine—you can tell because the boys
are drawing aliens on the place mats with sugar-crystal hair,

still moving forward, not yet dreaming in reverse,
trafficking in a brotherhood that promises never to end,
and when "Strawberry Fields" fades down to street noise,

Jackson asks, *Which Beatle sings that one, Dad?*
And Sam says, *John Lennon.*
And Jackson says, *Idiot—everybody knows John Lennon is dead.*

CAPITALIST POEM #57

Like a sailor practicing knots in the darkness,
like a warrior sharpening his blade in the lull of battle,
like a blind man searching out the figure of a sleeping lover

the mind surges and eddies
through the concourses of the terminal
with its way stations and concessions

of bottled water sandwiches,
dot.com billboards trumpeting instant riches,
another gourmet coffee at the cappuccino bar,

grande decaf half-skim latte,
seeking to delimit its appetites and hungers,
as even *Money* magazine wonders

how much is enough?
Like one returned home after years of hard travel
I call out in greeting to my familiars—

Avarice, trusted and faithful retainer,
Extravagance, *mi compañero,*
Greed, my old friend, my bodyguard, my brother.

THE MANATEE

Deep sunk in the dreamtime of his terminal coma,
the manatee persists like a vegetative outpatient,
victim of the whirling propellers of impatience
and a buoyantly bovine quiescence gone nova.

Dream deep, brother. Dream long and deep, sister sea cow.
May millennia of soft tides and sea grass sustain thy sleep
across the dark ages of extinction. May your memory keep
heavy the hearts and hulls of your inheritors. Us, for now.

STORM VALEDICTION

That sound is the thrashing of paper lanterns against the eaves.
Vessels frail as bodies lit with incandescent blood,
what else but that to survive the storm? What else could there be
to hold back the darkening rain of the city, empathy
like an opal, sorrow like a shriveled raisin
in the dust beneath the stove
but still a raisin. Pockets of odd coins, lint
to speak for transience and the rusted metal of fallen leaves,
paper cups with pastel scrimshaw elephants or diamonds, whatever
yolk the dawn subscribes for our delectation,
whatever throne the night sees fit to claim from the angels.
Difficult, difficult. All of it, any of it—
schoolgirls, vendors of sunglasses, businessmen
trembling their woes toward destiny and sleep—to feel it
or perish in the wicks of unlit candles,
to begin again within the inked shells of Easter eggs.
Steam is rising from grates, a child
pedals a bicycle through the alleyway of ghosts unafraid.
Purity, the maw of it, blackbirds and kestrels
against a sky the color of antique mahjong tiles, color of aspirin
dissolving in seawater as the sun bursts its amnion
of tattered clouds like the raw carcass of the heart revealed.
That sound is the ticking of paper lanterns in the storm.
Just that. It is hard
in the radiance of this world to live
but we live.

ROCK FALLS, ILLINOIS

Now the clouds are pleasure craft and tugboats towing strings of
    empties across the mighty Mississippi.
Now we're singing "Ring of Fire" as we slough past scrap-wood
    shacks strung high along the levee,
regiments of willow shoots, phalanxes of cottonwood among the
    islets and sandy channels,
backwater mudflats papered in drowned Nilotic reeds with
    seedpods rattling in empty sockets
like Babylonian baby toys, like the stork and ibis amulets of ancient
    Sumerian funerary wands.
Now the palisades are waving kindled branches in warning. Now
    the local flocks: crow, duck, grackle.
Now the night has shed its skin and taken root, alluvial soil two
    hundred feet deep, black earth overturned
as the ungainly reapers ratcheting dry stalks to husk-mulch and
    grain clip through the dusty acres of sheaves.
Now Patty Loveless is on the radio. Now the annual interstate game
    with the ritual rival across the river.
Now squadrons of geese settle to the stubble field, bushels of apples
    and butternut squash,
hay bales, clover honey, scarecrows bearing pumpkins and cider to
    scavenge the empty miles of silos.
Now the country music station from De Kalb or Clinton begins to
    falter as we come to the first sure sign of the city,
road deconstruction, cigarettes and lotto tickets, two-lanes of
    jackhammered arterial funnel
to choke the reek of mini-marts and muffler shops back to the long-
    corrupted aorta.
Now the mills like skeletons of prehistoric whales in the distance.
Now the familiar planetary gloom of a pancake house orbiting
    against ectopic eclipse,
waiters trundling gurneys of blueberry syrup like doctors delivering
    a miracle serum

to the lone patient left alive inside the Belgian waffle ward. Now the
old neighborhoods of the millworkers,
blue-domed churches and backyard shrines, shuttered taverns and
Union Halls,
blocks of wooden bungalows with old-world flags and used car
dealers flying patriotic bunting.
Now the upturned cobbles are cast against the ice machine behind
the liquor store.
Now the country music is lost altogether. Now we too are lost
among the mills and foundries collapsing in decay,
brickyards and crucibles, husks the size of aircraft hangars full of
desolate machinery
like the ruins of ancient siege engines or prized displays at a trade
show or ghostly exhibition,
the Great Hall of Abandoned Dreams. Now the road expires in
barbed wire and tangled thickets,
the bridge a ruin of joists and wishbones in the weeds and broken
cinder blocks below,
the Rock River rife with trash and spoil like an animal slit open by
hunters to spill the foam and spoor of its entrails.
Now the forsaken freight tracks lead nowhere. Now grocery carts
are wheeled across the empty lots
by the hands of invisible shoppers gloved in fallen leaves. Now the
clouds are barges full of salt.

THE FLY

As for the fly I chased around the bathroom with a towel that night,
    swatting, slapping, thrashing, pounding,
kicking with one foot the toothbrush cup onto its side, dislodging
    the tea curtain with a misplaced elbow,
unable for all my efforts to terminate his gallant loops and
    arabesques, his beeline dives and fighter-pilot vectorings,
his stalls and silences, his crafty retreats, his increasingly erratic
    bursts toward any open corner or avenue of escape,
behind the toilet, above the shower rod, inside the light wells,
    disappearing like a magician only to reappear again and again—
as for the fly, our struggle went on a long time. Too long. It was
    already after midnight when it began, the house calm,
everything dark beyond our gladiatorial arena, crazy to bother,
    ridiculous to carry on, but I was determined to finish it.

And when he stopped at last, gone for good, the body unseen
    but certainly dead, pulverized at a blow, squashed and
    unrecoverable,
when that silence was assured I felt certain of a conquest too small
    to call a triumph but a victory nonetheless.

And when, the next day, lifting a fresh towel from the bar, he fell to
    the floor, not dead but irreparably damaged,
lurching, toppling, lopsided, wing-still, no longer jittering with
    defiance, no longer challenging fate with desperate brio,
when I discovered him then everything had changed, and we were
    no longer fated to deadly opposition,
no longer entranced by the simplicity of our struggle, and I no
    longer understood the antagonism of the night before,

felt entirely alien from it, felt now that it was a perturbing frenzy, a
    kind of madness that had possessed me.

Which did not mean that he did not have to die, only that it was
        not, or not anymore, an act of murder but a cost of war,
or so I told myself, adorned in the common skin of my kind, naked
    before the mirror in the exalted light of morning.

ZEUGMA

Zeugma. From the Greek, *zeugnynai,* to join together; from
        a pair of animals linked at labor;
yoked oxen. The Greeks, of course, for whom beginnings signified
        better than endings, alpha & omega, for whom
x was just another letter: xiphoid, xerophagy, xenophobia, xoanon.
        Civilization, perforce, is abecedarian.
When Xenophon's hoplites charged the Persians at Cunaxa he
        denied the agency of local gods, mistaking
vox populi for *vox angelica,* voice of a suffering populace
        entirely freed of fleshly yoke,
uplifted in exquisite agony. Such are the costs of transmigration.
        Fish demand ladders, wooden horses
transhumance, referring to reindeer but apropos in Ilium,
        green-fingered Lydia or Mesopotamia,
stage for the tidal clash of cultures & languages, ebbs & floods
        hardly unique to Persians & Greeks.
Recall the illiterate Pizarro against the hummingbird-feathered
        Inca Atahualpa, sun-god & moon-
queen trampled into Andean dust by a few dozen Spaniards
        jointly with their horses, gunpowder, &
priestly blessing to sanctify such slaughter in the name of the king of
        kings. Back to Xenophon & the Ten Thousand:
on the retreat now, following the Tigris, they come to a ruined city,
        Larissa, inhabited by Medes, thought to be
none other than Nimrud, ancient Kalhu, hippogriffs become
        Medean in the wake of serial conquest,
median point on their march from Babylon toward the hills of Armenia,
        none cheered by that barren vision, dire
Larissa, omen of defeat, citadel of political impermanence.
        On the next day, great Nineveh, abandoned:
kings, seneschals, satraps, jesters, fletchers, peltasts, potters,
        priestly & noble classes—vanished con-

jointly into equitable oblivion, weaver & wool, smith & tool,
      queen & fool. So much for the Assyrians.
Ink, a luxury, so no texts but wind-scoured stone remain to help us
      recall them, our contemporary ignorance
hardly less monumental than Xenophon's self-serving chronicle,
      scene by scene inventing ancient history.
Green no longer, that Fertile Crescent, mislabeled by an en-
      tranced human stab at metaphoric order.
Fish into amphibians, logograms into syllabaries, seas into lands
      uplifted in autochthonic agons
entirely unwitnessed, template free of cartographic correlatives,
      vox barbara or *vox nihili,* celestial music
denied in our fury to claim an alphabet forged from the metals of chaos.
      When the ox moves, the plow moves.
Civilization, perforce, is boustrophedonic: *x-y-z; z-y-*
      x. Better the blue mud of the Euphrates,
better the raw ore of belief than these chains of syntax, this
      yoke of definitions. Xoanon:
a primitive idol resembling the rough block from which it was carved.
      Zeugma: maker & vessel, master & slave.

EGYPTOLOGY

Even in that hour the knowledge
that our willful titanism cannot save us,
such prescient constructs no more
than ribbons time itself has braided
in our hair, courses of the river in flood
season after season rewritten
while bedrock glistens unperturbed.

Even chiseled, hawsered, sawn into blocks,
stacked, girdered, engineered, blessed,
it is no more than a division of spoils,
partitions of a hive which may yet
be thrown down from its perch
and burned in coils of scented smoke,
moonfall bitten blue and amoral
across the marmoreal sky
of a descent beyond reckoning,
baubles, buried treasure, canopic jars,
lost process by which we shall know
no home but eternity, no balm
but sweet water in the shade of date palms,
a ringing of earthenware bells,
small foundries forging ingots of tin,
oil lamps along the water where
boys on donkeys proffer cinnamon and figs
beside the granary of the Pharaoh.

Because it lives here, within us, has burned
its fingerprints into the fabric of stars
unspooled from the spinnerets of time
the spider, time the jackal, the ass,
time the healer, the embalmer, the annealer,
the anointer, the vain and destructive,

the intransigent, the incorporeal, the just,
the praiseworthy, the bereaving and bereft—

always the same, witness and vanishing,
ransacked, laid bare, scoured, thirsty,
incorruptible and transformed and always

the same.

We cannot touch it, halt it, name it.

It sails past, wind upon the Nile,
rowed by whom and bound for what shore?

THE TOAD

In the courtyard of our house there is a fountain
in the form of a whitewashed dolphin
leaping from a scalloped, algae-ridden bowl
in which a rag-eared antler of stag coral sits bleaching.

The sun here is fierce enough to burn away the water
in three or four days, and this morning
I am tasked to fill it again, and to clear the small pump
of fallen leaves and allamanda blossoms,

feeling weary, hollowed out, frayed and startled
enough to drop the watering can with a jolt
at the tingling signal of an animal presence,
the sudden awareness of another living creature at hand,

that sensory aura or electrical field felt
and recognized by some nerve-kernel of the brain
undiscarded through all our baroque evolution.
It is a toad. Big as my fist, cloud-gray,

its rubbery head emerging from the fountain's murk
like a weird, grinning, operatic goblin mask.
When it blinks the camera lenses of its uncanny eyes
I can see that they are gold, brilliant and metallic,

like moon-lander foil hammered over robotic orbs.
My heart is pounding like a piston,
like the fine hammer of that goldsmith. It aches
profoundly as a torn bicep. All week I have been lashed

and scoured by an ocean of phantoms
and I am worn smooth as beach glass,

deeply exhausted, and more
than a little bit lost.

Faster and faster our children are disappearing
into the mist of the future
even as we shout into our parents' ears
to remind them of the past. Do you remember it,

father? Do you?

More than ever I lean upon Elizabeth,
like the clothes of a scarecrow upon its staff.

My cloak to ward the rain from her skin.
My hat to fend the sun from her brow.
My crooked smile to scatter the grackles.

Do you remember, father?
Do you remember any of it—

the steep slate roof on which the trees
rained down their hoard of summer acorns—

a green station wagon skating an exit ramp
into the icy meadow of a clover leaf
in slow motion, unstoppable, unharmed—

a picnic by a ruined mill
where three mountain streams converged—

where was that place, can you tell me,
do you remember?

Yes, I remember—it was long ago, in Italy.

You were a child and I carried you up the mountain
and you swam with your brother in the pools
of melted snow run down from the Alps to the millpond
past dark hill towns like the dwellings of trolls,
older than the Romans, much older,
and I swam beside you in the ice-green water,
and rested on hot boulders in the sunshine,
the muscles of my back grew warm as the ropes of a sailboat,
I was strong, your mother was beautiful,
we ate bread and cheese where a fig tree
burdened the soil with its wild, discarded seeds,
we walked up the stream, collecting stones,
floating sticks over tiny cataracts,
we startled a toad from a rock and watched it
struggle to swim away, paddling its elastic arms
and bowing its webbed legs against the current
to hold its place exactly,
neither moving forward nor slipping back,
a strange, knobbed, ancient creature,
like the unlucky prince transformed by an ogre,
like the king of the mountain in disguise,
and when we rescued him, exhausted, to the grassy bank,
what was it he whispered to me alone?

I am neither prince nor troll
nor toad
but time itself.

Every instant of your existence
belongs to me
but I give you this moment as my gift.

Remember this day, this hour, this very second.
Guard it well.
Keep it as I would keep it.

For when next you see me
know that I have come to reclaim
what you have failed to treasure sufficiently.

Know that my realm is eternal and inhuman.
Know that I am merciless.
Know me by my golden eyes.

SHRIMP BOATS, BILOXI

These wings, these lights, this shoal of angels
sieved against the gulf, gull-bent
arks of the high dusk
waters, arm in arm, rippled and linked
in their slow patrol
and orbit, the fleet, the nets,
the numerals
from which our days evolve,
wave-battered, moon-betrayed, fluid
as silk. Still
the moment
impends. A father and son
are trolling the shallows
for mullet, knee-deep beneath the pillared
dream of the interstate engineers
at neap tide. The black-
jacketed Baptists down from the convention
center for coffee and fried
oysters preach amazing
grace the gospel of life hereafter
as they distribute
refrigerator
magnets, but those who attend
the keening dorsals
are none so
certain, I mean the dolphins'
jeremiad, milky tiger
lilies speaking in tongues, wind-shuck
of the exhausted flocks, oil
rigs and pelicans and harbor-craft
on Mobile Bay, shiver
and rock
of the voyage out,

the journey
in, I mean
the rage of faith,
I mean the light-storm, blind
drunk on the oceanic
surge, I mean
the jerks, the shakes, the waves'
lupercalia,
the blue seizures
of noon. Sweet
sugar of life
deliver me the means
to fix, grant me the music,
the salt, the song. Vast rapture of this world
bear me with the wings and candles
of your chosen
vessels, number me
among that company,
raise me high upon your darkening
harmony. Tide, wind, spirit
take me up
in these rags of twilight.

THEN

What happens then, after the stars explode, after the universe
    expands to the limits of possibility,
after the bones of the last animals disappear into the plains, and
    melt into the dirt, and rise up as corn,
rise up as grass blowing in the autumn winds that carry the soil
    back to the sea as the oceans boil away
and the galaxies recoil into swirling matter, and the earth becomes
    a single ripple, a single integer in that equation?

What happens then, how does the story turn out, the social
    narratives in many languages, the striving cultures,
new definitions of justice, new plans for a rebuilt city, leaders and
    followers, a championship season,
plots and dramas we each have played our small part in, our
    domestic sentence, our phrase or motif,
our single character—& or q—whichever shape our being has
    pressed into the ledger of time?

What happens after our works have all been forgotten, the
    paintings lost, the architecture collapsed,
when the last books have fallen into the sea to be consumed by
    whales, digested by shrimp and minnows,
when our music no longer echoes, and lampreys alone read the
    poetry of humanity in the dim library of the deep?

What happens after the body fails, after the noise of the blood falls
    still, the lungs grow stiff,
after the white bird ascends from the marsh at dawn to escort the
    soul to the borders of this realm,
the day, the hour, the moment after—what happens then, what
    happens then?

LUXURY

Word-skeins,
ropes of language, flaxen cordage,
what luxury to coil its supple circumference

in spools, rolls, bobbins, reels,
weaving and looping, knotting, untangling,
slipping a blade to its fibers—

instead of history this entitlement,
this private wonder,
this poem.

CAMPBELL McGRATH

Thumbing the road atlas, I imagine that ultimate voyage,
transcontinental, multinational, taken the long way on the
     diagonal,
Florida to Alaska, because there are many Campbells
but only one McGrath, and it is there, arrow in the heart of the
     wilderness
beyond Denali, beyond the cold waters of the Kuskokwim where
the last and farthest roads give way to ruts and tracks
across the tundra, snow and distance, a vastness, an emptiness,
     never-ending.
Unfathomable road trip. Frigid, Stygian destination.
And a beginning, here and now, raveled twine humid and umbilical,
point of embarkation for the labyrinth of the nominal,
here and now, in hot and floral Campbell, Florida,
west of Kissimmee, south of Orlando, then north to encounter
the next most proximal, cleaving the concave condo banana
and the Marshes of Glynn across Georgia to Savannah,
and through the piney woods of Caroline, 77 all the way to
     Wytheville,
then into the deepest darkest of the wild and wonderful,
West Virginia, country roads and toothless ancients, carry me home
to Appalachia, and a trestle over the river to Campbell, Ohio,
subsumed by Youngstown, cold-rolled corridor of steel and
     abandonment,
now west and south, up, up and away, slag and ash supplanted
by bluegrass, and across the Mississippi at Finley to Campbell,
     Missouri,
earthworm spoonhandled in the arms of the flooded muddy,
not far from Braggadocio, Current View, or Hayti,
then southwest through Pocahontas, Campbell Station and
     Arkadelphia,
Arkansas, bound for the land of Matador and Lone Star,
asphalt beeline direct for Campbell, kin to Commerce,

colossus astraddle Route 66, midway betwixt Dallas and Paris,
then drive all day to get out of Texas, arid and blameless, enough
   said
about that sadness, Roswell, Flagstaff, even Las Vegas,
bitter coagulant blood from a stone, into the vale of borax and bone
and up the west slope of the Sierra Nevada and down
again through the ghost towns of gold country,
north of Yosemite, down to the boundless oasis of the valley,
silver aqueduct of dreams and fertility, south through Lodi,
stemming the grapevine from Patterson to San Jose,
shadow of the Bay and silicon suburbia, sweet, sweet Campbell,
   California,
last of the first on that golden coast, that homonymic host,
lest we forget a slew of sibling claimants, various and variant,
Campbellsport, Wisconsin, Campbellsville and Campbellsburg,
   Kentucky,
and Campbellsburg, Indiana, sister city settled by emigrants
in a meadow of yarrow and horse-high hay,
and fields of rusted cars outside Campbellstown, PA,
and not just townships and municipalities but even the counties,
as again in Kentucky, heart of the mighty Campbell country,
and north again, farther north, across the border and all over
   Canada,
Campbellton, Campbellford, Campbell's Bay, the great Campbell
   River,
on Vancouver Island, whence carted by orcas across the black waters
and back to the mainland at Bella Coola, British Columbia,
and up the oily scrim of the Alcan through Vanderhoof and
   Hazelton,
Whitehorse where the boom once was, and into Alaska
to complete the equation, cruising the blacktop on moosewatch to
   Fairbanks,
a road of summer gravel through Chatanika to Eureka,

along the Tanana, and the vast ice artery of the heartless Yukon,
by ferry to a hardscrabble roadhead of washboard near Ruby,
through Long Creek down to Poorman, wary animals in the alder
    scrub
and smell of rancid chicken blood and vague directions south,
into the emptiness, toward the headwaters of the primitive
    Nowitna,
permafrost spun to mud along the last miles of navigable tirehold,
thickets of brush and intractable scree, chill of dusk in the embers'
    lees,
constellated ashes, glacial till, light in the distance could be fox fire
or sign of an early aurora, skirl of tundra and guessed-at ranges,
snow dragging with it the whiteness of the interior,
white quadrants of impersonal destiny, beyond any known
    boundary
of the geological survey, where the atlas surrenders its horn of
    hooded inklings
and mute words are limned in the halo-glimmer of the nameless,
and the dogs howl in their traces, and the sled path disintegrates
to chalk-track ellipses. . . . All maps are useless now.
These final steps must be taken alone, like the ragged first footfalls
of some yolk and caul hatchling along a wild river,
in the woods, at the foot of the mountains, in a valley of stars,
beyond vehicle of the familiar, language or skin,
in the darkness without and the darkness within.
There, where the road ends, the real journey begins.